D0290607

From Youth to Constructive Adult Life

THE NATIONAL SOCIETY
FOR THE STUDY OF EDUCATION

Series on Contemporary Educational Issues
Kenneth J. Rehage, Series Editor

The 1978 Titles

History, Education and Public Policy: Recovering the American Educational Past, Donald R. Warren, Editor
Aspects of Reading Education, Susanna Pflaum-Connor, Editor
From Youth to Constructive Adult Life: The Role of the Public School, Ralph W. Tyler, Editor

The National Society for the Study of Education also publishes Yearbooks which are distributed by the University of Chicago Press. Inquiries regarding all publications of the Society, as well as inquiries about membership in the Society, may be addressed to the Secretary-Treasurer, 5835 Kimbark Avenue, Chicago, IL 60637. Membership in the Society is open to any who are interested in promoting the investigation and discussion of educational questions.

From Youth to Constructive Adult Life: The Role of the Public School

Edited by

Ralph W. Tyler

Director Emeritus of
the Center for Advanced Study
in the Behavioral Sciences

McCutchan Publishing Corporation
2526 Grove Street
Berkeley, California 94704

ISBN 0-8211-1907-9
Library of Congress Catalog Card Number 77-95249

Printed in the United States of America

Series Foreword

The publications of the National Society for the Study of Education in its 1978 Series on Contemporary Educational Issues include three volumes that deal with major and continuing concerns of the educational profession. This volume, *From Youth to Constructive Adult Life: The Role of the Public School,* focuses on issues that are receiving a considerable amount of attention in a period when the transition from youth to responsible adulthood appears to be increasingly difficult for many young people.

Ralph W. Tyler, editor of this volume, has devoted much of his long and distinguished career to analyzing the role of the school in the context of the pervasive social forces that affect education. Two decades ago he was asked to provide the leadership in the preparation of a volume, *Social Forces Influencing American Education,* which appeared in 1961 as Part II of the Society's Sixtieth Yearbook. It is indicative of his continuing interest in these matters and of his particularly genuine concern for youth that he arranged for the conference, held under the auspices of the Center for the Study of Democratic Institutions, at which many of the papers included in this volume were presented.

The Society is grateful that Dr. Tyler has made the papers available for publication and appreciates his invaluable assistance in the editing of them. We also recognize the efforts of the several authors, whose varied perspectives on the problems to which this book is addressed provide insights that should be enormously helpful in understanding the problems involved.

Kenneth J. Rehage

for the Committee on an Expanded
Publication Program of the
National Society for the Study
of Education

Preface

Concern for young people making the transition from adolescence to adulthood in the United States has increased over the past ten years. Opportunities for gradually assuming adult responsibilities, for participating with adults in a manner that engenders confidence in the ability of the young to take on adult roles, and for rendering meaningful service to others appear, it would seem, to be diminishing. Reports on these problems have been published by several different organizations, but there has been no comprehensive outline of the educational issues involved; nor have any examples of ways in which schools might resolve the problem been set forth.

Recognizing the need for a discussion of this problem by school personnel, parents, scholars, and representatives from business, government, and the professions, the Center for the Study of Democratic Institutions sponsored a conference on the subject that was generously supported by the Illinois Humanities Council. All but four of the chapters in this volume were prepared as a result of this conference, which was held in March 1976.

In October of that same year, the Center also cooperated with the University of Minnesota's Center for Youth Development and Research to hold a one-day conference at the Spring Hill Conference Center in Wayzata, Minnesota. This second conference was intended to initiate local planning for youth employment, and the chapters by Paul Barton and Ralph Tyler were initially prepared to give direction to that effort.

The two conferences were followed by a Center Dialogue in Chicago in February 1977. The chapter written by Stephen Bailey was intended to stimulate interdisciplinary discussion in that dialogue. The final chapter, written by Donald Eberly, originally appeared in *Social Policy*. It is included in this volume because his suggestions differ in some important respects from those in the other chapters and because a national service act is now being debated by the federal government.

These fifteen chapters, taken together, furnish an in-depth examination of the problems young people face as they move toward adult life and suggest how schools might be able to help. No other single volume provides such a comprehensive view.

Several of the contributions that appear here are reprinted from *The Center Magazine*. The conferences and the dialogues were also recorded. Edited tapes are available from the Center for the Study of Democratic Institutions, Box 4068, Santa Barbara, California, 93103.

Chicago
September 1, 1977

Ralph W. Tyler

Contributors

Stephen K. Bailey, Professor of Education and Social Policy, Harvard University

Paul E. Barton, Senior Associate, National Manpower Institute

Harry S. Broudy, Professor Emeritus of Philosophy and of Education, University of Illinois (Champaign-Urbana)

James S. Coleman, Professor of Sociology, University of Chicago

Bruce Dollar, Staff Associate, National Commission on Resources for Youth

Elizabeth Douvan, Professor of Psychology, University of Michigan (Ann Arbor)

Donald J. Eberly, Executive Director, National Service Secretariat

Edwin Fenton, Professor of History and Director, Carnegie-Mellon Education Center, Carnegie-Mellon University

Jacob W. Getzels, Professor of Education and of the Behavioral Sciences, University of Chicago

Robert J. Havighurst, Professor Emeritus of Education and of the Behavioral Sciences, University of Chicago

Diane Hedin, Assistant Director, Center for Youth Development and Research, University of Minnesota

Mary Conway Kohler, Executive Director, National Commission on Resources for Youth

Byron Schneider, Principal, Southwest Secondary School, Minneapolis, Minnesota

Edwin Schneider, Assistant Superintendent, Portland (Oregon) Public Schools

Joseph J. Schwab, Associate, Center for the Study of Democratic Institutions, and Professor Emeritus of Natural Sciences in the College and Professor Emeritus of Education, University of Chicago

Ralph W. Tyler, Director Emeritus, Center for Advanced Study in the Behavioral Sciences and Director of the Chicago Program, Center for the Study of Democratic Institutions

Contents

PART ONE
From Youth to Adulthood: Problems in Socialization

1. A Proper Preparation: Historical Perspectives on Schools and Socialization in America

Donald R. Warren

The common school, Henry Barnard argued in 1839, must offer a "proper preparation for the real business of life."[1] For him, that reality consisted of the world of work, social membership, and political participation, and proper preparation would necessarily be practical, not abstract or "bookish." Literacy, a basic and common morality, and national loyalty were the goals that, alone, could promise individual freedom and national growth, and, without them, the nation would pay a heavy price in terms of disunity and conflict. Incompetent and immoral leaders would be elected by illiterate and naive citizens unable or unwilling to earn their own livelihood. Individuals had to be free to escape from the common horde, the accidents of low birth, and the political slavery that uneducated voters might impose on themselves. Success, to be sure, required more than good schools. Those, Barnard concluded, could be found in Europe, but their effect was "depressed" by fixed law, iron custom, and "repressive despotic government."[2] American schoolchildren, even with half-trained teachers, abbreviated school terms, unsystematic curricula, and dilapidated, one-room schoolhouses had the advantage of a free press, the chance to elect leaders and shape laws, and opportunities to chart their individual futures. Capitalizing on these opportunities required effective preparation, which rendered even more imperative the need for public education.

Over a half-century later, William T. Harris, near the close of his long tenure as United States Commissioner of Education, voiced similar expectations and goals.[3] By 1898, however, he could punctuate them with statistics of achievement. For Harris, the greatest accomplishment of the public schools was the transformation of an illiterate population into a people "that reads the newspaper and thinks on national and international interests." In the cities he could point to large, graded schools that taught "regularity, punctuality, silence, and conformity to order—military drill." Simply because of their size and complexity, large, urban schools, unlike small, rural ones, required that such lessons be learned well. But students also benefited directly by being thus prepared for participation in urban society and the "age of productive industry." In such schools, the student learned "to hold back his animal impulses" and to join in "concerted action," lessons important for citizenship that also had "military significance." Discipline was viewed as being important for "self-government." Given conditions at the turn of the century, Harris concluded, "the city school is a stronger moral force [than the rural school] because of its superior training in regularity, punctuality, orderly concerted action, and self-restraint." It produced self-respect because it taught students not merely to read but also "to criticize" what they read and helped them to avoid crime, vice, and illiteracy. Harris, however, cautioned against exaggerated claims. "School education is not a cause but an index of orderly tendencies in the family." It was the "auxiliary institution founded for the purpose of reinforcing the education of the four fundamental institutions of civilization: family, civil society . . . , state, church."[4]

With some pride, Harris charted evidence of the school's growing strength as index and reinforcer.[5] The proportion of children five to eighteen years of age enrolled in common schools rose from 61.45 percent in 1870 to 70.08 percent in 1897. The most spectacular gains occurred in the South Atlantic states (from 30.51 to 63.63 percent), the South Central states (from 34.17 to 64.41 percent), and the Western states (from 54.77 to 76.73 percent). The ratio of students in average daily attendance to the total number enrolled rose from 60.1 to 68.4 during this period, and the average number of days that each enrolled student attended classes increased from 79.4 to 97.8. Perhaps these are modest achievements by late-twentieth-century standards, but in 1897 they represented solid accomplishment. Not all of the signs were positive. Of the school-age population in the North Atlantic states, the percentage actually enrolled in school dropped sharply from 1870 to

1897 (from 77.95 to 70.38 percent), and in the North Central states it hovered unsteadily at about 76 percent.

The expectations and rationales for public education that Barnard and Harris shared may strike late-twentieth-century observers as conservative.[6] Their views also encompass notions viewed as novel and prophetic today, and to this extent they represent a tradition of thought about education, particularly public education, that is still with us. They also illustrate a persistent theme: public schools have historically been expected to play a significant role in preparing the young, and some adults as well, for membership in society. One could argue, in fact, that socialization has been the dominant goal of the schools over the past two centuries.

SCHOOLS FOR PEOPLE—AND THE NATION

The more recent revisionist historians have insisted that what early school reformers proposed or envisioned is not as significant as what the schools actually accomplished. The revisionists claim that reality has fallen short of the ideal, and, even worse, that articulations of the educational dream masked attempts to render working-class Americans docile and uncritically obedient.

Although it has become fashionable to discount the "rhetoric of expectation" that accompanied the growth of American public schools in the nineteenth century, the rhetoric is still important.[7] It expresses an American commitment to education bordering on religious conviction that antedated the common school revival of the 1830s and 1840s. Even though, as the revisionists insist, articulations of the educational dream represent the bias of their authors, these were men and women committed to the growth of public schools, and their dream attracted an audience, for, by the end of the century the majority of school-age children were enrolled in public schools. The rhetoric may reveal little of what students found once they were enrolled, but it may help to explain why they made the effort to go to school.

The rhetoric reveals a curious and fundamental ambivalence that is especially clear in the writings of Benjamin Rush, and later in the works of Mann, Barnard, Harris, and Dewey. On the one hand, schools were perceived as agents of liberation and individual fulfillment, and, on the other, as strategies for building social cohesion and quelling "excessive individuality."[8] They were to be both guarantors of freedom and instruments of social control. The complexities of this ambivalence constitute the major difficulty in charting the history of public school socialization in the United States.

The most consistent theme throughout this history is the argument that schools are necessary in a democratic state. Here, too, ambivalence is evident. Echoing what had become a truism by 1840, Barnard insisted that free citizens could not enjoy their rights, including the franchise, without at least a basic literacy. Neither could the nation survive without intelligent voters and elected officials. To paraphrase Jefferson, this was not all the nation needed, but it needed at least this. It also required loyalty and a measure of tranquility among its various sections, classes, religions, and races. The school's responsibility became heavy indeed: to prepare citizens for practical freedom and to deliver to the nation a people welded by common loyalties and political values. It was also to promote domestic peace by offering common opportunities for training and learning. It was to serve as a staging area from which individuals left prepared for a vocation and, thereby, for economic advancement or at least security. It was by means of the public school that the nation might escape the turmoil of a French Revolution. When finally confronted with the reality of their own Civil War, they reacted as might be expected: secession and war could have been avoided if the South had shared the Union commitment to popular education.

The objectives were clear. Public schools were expected to provide basic learning, at least literacy, promote common values and citizenship, and develop the additional skills needed for employment and, as Barnard put it, "the real business of life." All of these were essentially socialization goals. When pushed, Horace Mann insisted that moral training was the most important responsibility of the common school, and it became an essential ingredient in the high school program, particularly the teacher-training department. By the close of the nineteenth century moral training was part of the established curriculum. Pedagogical efforts, as well as the organization and structure of the school itself, served to equip students with the virtues and attitudes they would need for adult roles in an urban, industrial society.

Then, early in the twentieth century, a new socialization strategy—the "extra curriculum"—surfaced. It provided the means for "total supervision of the students' social life."[9] The school was a society, concluded Frank Winslow Johnson of the University of Chicago Laboratory School, and the child a social being. His education was not preparation for life, but life itself. Johnson viewed the school, particularly the high school, as being better equipped than families or churches for bringing order to student sociability through adult supervision. The "proper preparation" of youth thus utilized all manner of clubs, activities, and athletic events, in addition to the academic curriculum, each "carefully" planned and supervised by teachers. Johnson especially favored student government, "this peculiar method of control," for its practical lessons in citizenship.[10] He cautioned against leaving it without the guidance of teachers, however, adding that it was "highly artificial" and hence potentially boring to students.

Earle Rugg agreed with Johnson that student government aided citizenship training and that it rendered obsolete such dated approaches as memorizing facts in civics classes.[11] Noting the widespread existence of student government in schools across the country, Rugg expected students to learn citizenship by behaving as citizens. Student participation in such activities, he argued, was a successful and worthy feature of the school, an intrinsic good. It also served as an aid to discipline, promoted schoolwork and school spirit, and fostered a cooperative spirit among faculty and students and a respect for law and order. Leonard Koos expanded these claims to encompass extracurricular activites in general.[12] He felt that such activities promoted the acquisition of civic, social, and moral values. These progressive innovations left untouched the socializing aims articulated for schools early in the nineteenth century; at best they invoked new strategies that retained the ambivalence evident in their predecessors.

Herbert Croly, a progressive of the Theodore Roosevelt school, offered his version of the persistent aims of American education and the underlying ambiguities that were still evident early in the twentieth century. Chastising Americans for their superstitious belief in education as a means for individual and social "uplift," Croly nonetheless insisted that education constituted "the real vehicle of improvement" that prepared individuals with the resolve and tools needed to pursue their objectives.[13] Likewise, it prepared them for the concerted action needed to pursue repetitiously and experimentally the national purposes. In each case, purpose served as the liberating factor. Without it, neither the individual nor the nation was free to realize its potential. Properly prepared and disciplined, individuals could attain their own liberation and contribute to that of their country through pursuit of national ideals, a task necessarily experimental and recurring for each generation. Education was not a direct means to, say, a better job; rather, it represented an attempt to resolve conflicts between individual aspiration and the nation's need for social cohesion. Individual emancipation followed as a function of collective membership. In acquiring "social education," individuals were actually helped by the as yet unfulfilled promise of the nation. The nation offered the individual "a really formative and inspiring opportunity for public service."[14] In this curious way, education became an intermediate step in the political and economic reconstruction of the country.

One can understand why Croly roused the ire of radical revisionists among historians of education.[15] Although he offered a thorough critique of educational practices at the time, he also reiterated the basic tenets of nineteenth-century public school advocates. These can be reduced to two: for the sake of individuals and society, public education must be enforced, and it must be inclusive. Together, these beliefs provide the earliest conception of equal educational opportunity in the United States. The rationale for compulsory school attendance began to be articulated late in the eighteenth century by Benjamin Rush, Noah Webster, and others. Confronted with their own assertions of the necessity of education for the well-being of both individuals and the nation, common school reformers in the 1840s and 1850s argued that children must be schooled, by entreaty if possible or by legislative mandate if it came to that. Furthermore, not some but all of the youth were to be included. Public education had to be common.

THE LURE OF HOMOGENEITY: PATTERNS OF EXCLUSION

The effects of this concept of equal educational opportunity touched succeeding generations of Americans. It informed the rationales supporting public schools for black people early in the antebellum years and education policy imposed on the South during Reconstruction. It was a part of the promise to immigrants and the basis for demanding inclusive and integrated public schools for blacks during the twentieth century. Over the years, it has influenced Americans generally to expect education as a right, despite the fact that no such guarantee appears in the Constitution of the United States and the ideal has yet to be realized.

The history of American education has been written emphasizing the rhetoric of expectation. The story can also detail instances of exclusion and inequality. Some historians argue that the exclusions have been deliberate, for, within the confines of school policy, patterns of direct and indirect barriers to inclusion can be detected. Black people and Native Americans have been victimized by patently intentional exclusions. The indirect barriers present a different kind of problem. In such cases, exclusion has often taken subtle forms, ranging from the use of textbooks with an anti-Catholic bias for children of Catholic immigrants to the tracking of students in programs or schools segregated by race, social class, or ethnicity. Evidence attesting the effects of such policies on the children and parents who experienced them is still being gathered, but one can conclude that the policies promised are at best prepartion for limited social membership.

Of the forms of indirect exclusion, two evolved from the original concept of equal educational opportunity: one related to enforcement of education; the other, to the goal of commonality. Common school reformers from Horace Mann in the 1840s to Ohio's Emerson White in the 1860s spoke of a "law of external force," which, according to White, best explained the growth of American public education. The law derived from the necessity of enforcing education for the sake of individuals and the nation. Unable to tolerate ignorance among its citizens, the nation had a clear stake in their education. Here is where the reformers encountered difficulties. How could ignorant people be expected to promote and plan their own enlightenment? The answer, of course, was that they could not. Needed, therefore, were external forces in the form of state legislation and agencies and educational professionals to provide the necessary pressure. The centralization and professionalization of public education, which surfaced as major reform efforts late in the nineteenth century, had their beginnings much earlier. And they resulted in a powerful form of exclusion: exclusion from participation in school control and policymaking. As noted above, early twentieth-century progressives offered a partial and cautious corrective by moving to incorporate student participation in the school society. It was an effort at more effective socialization.

The second form of indirect exclusion that evolved from the concept of equal educational opportunity originated from defining commonality as sameness. The lure of homogeneity had attracted support for public education since the nation began. In the early national period public education was endorsed as a nation-building strategy. One of its contributions would be, in George Washington's words, "the assimilation of the principles, opinions, and manners" of the American people.[16] "The more homogeneous our citizens can become," he concluded, "the greater will be our prospect of permanent union." A later generation watched apprehensively the growth of pluralistic urban centers and the influx of Irish Catholic immigrants. It seemed obvious to Calvin Stowe in the 1830s "that the foreigners who settle on our soil should cease to be Europeans and become Americans . . . and it must be our [the schoolmen's] great endeavor to effect this object so desirable and so necessary to our American welfare."[17] Neither isolated nor uncommon, such observations rested, perhaps unknowingly, on the assumption that cultural plurality implied disunion or, worse, disloyalty.

The Americanization of immigrants constituted deliberate policy, and it was a major assignment of nineteenth-century public schools. For some, "melting pot" strategies represented humane efforts to equip immigrant children for American life; for others, they were at least tacit acknowledgment of cultural inferiority. In any case, as Gregory Mason argued in 1916, the loyalties and understandings of immigrants must be firmly established: "Hyphenated citizenship is as dangerous to the republic as a cancer to the human body. Education is the knife to use in cutting out the hyphen . . . ."[18] The particular strategies employed by the schools included bilingual programs in various cities throughout the nineteenth century, as well as adult education. The former tended to be viewed as temporary measures which could cease once the immigrant group began to advance toward assimilation. Such was the case in St. Louis.[19]

Americanization in schools provided a practical avenue for including immigrants in their new society. It was this, even when it took crude judgmental forms. But it was also a means for indirect exclusion through the rejection of cultural pluralism as a learning resource. Consider that, where bilingual programs flourished, bilingualism was rarely acknowledged as an intrinsic good. However understandable within the context of the times, the point was to eliminate "foreign" influences. This became particularly evident in the late nineteenth and early twentieth centuries, when a veritable flood of Eastern and Southern Europeans entered.

OUTCOMES: PREPARING YOUTH FOR ADULTHOOD

One is hard pressed, today, to find new socialization imperatives or novel conceptions of effective strategies. The issues that exercise us tend to recall unfinished debates in the past. Fears that youth in the 1970s are isolated and overinstitutionalized support proposals for new forms of apprenticeship, for learning alongside adults in the world of work. Henry Barnard endorsed such efforts in relation to the development of technical and vocational schools. Later, in the progressive era, similar proposals came from William George who thought his "Junior Republic" sounded the appropriate anti-institutional note for correcting the effect of schools in separating youth from adults and from "real life."[20] As a matter of course, he opposed legislative and constitutional proscriptions of child labor. Bilingual and ethnic studies programs employed as devices for socializing marginal youth surfaced not during the 1960s but more than a century earlier. Common school advocates held firm to the conviction that public schooling promised reductions in crime and poverty, and in 1965 apparently Lyndon Johnson did, too.[21] If Patrick Moynihan can complain that such expectations border on the fantastic, urging support for basic educational research to guide intelligent school objectives and policies, he may take comfort in similar recommendations from Emerson White in the 1860s.[22]

Schools as socializing institutions have changed, and new programs and socialization strategies have appeared, including the rise of vocational education in the early twentieth century. But the concern over the transition from youth to adulthood expressed by an older generation remains. History may serve in assessing past socializing efforts by the schools and, in the process, shed light on their potential roles in addressing the current youth problem. There is, however, an initial difficulty related to the data to be used. Historical evidence on the socializing effects of school from students' perspectives is difficult to find. This problem may eventually diminish with the help of interview data being gathered by historians, biographical research, and analytical tools borrowed from social and behavioral scientists, but, for the present, such disparate sources as popular literature, newspaper reports, and school census and demographic data must suffice.[23]

It is also necessary to set past roles of schools in their historical contexts. During the nineteenth century, according to Stephen Thernstrom, in large and small communities across the country roughly 50 percent of the people moved to other regions in any given decade.[24] This fact alone, which held constant across social-class lines, indicates considerable disruption in any school's socialization program and cautions against exaggerating the impact of those programs on students.

The effects of schooling have been weakened by external influences over which schools have had little control. Discriminatory hiring practices directed against immigrant workers were common. It was also true that rates of pay, particularly for unskilled laborers and industrial workers, frequently varied according to employees' national origins, with Southern and Eastern Europeans typically falling at the bottom of the scale. Such "realities" in the job market offered little positive encouragement to immigrant children hoping for occupational benefits from schooling.

Cultural factors as well explain some differences in educational attainment and job mobility among selected immigrant groups. Russian Jews succeeded in school and experienced considerable social mobility, whereas Irish and Southern Italians did not. The reasons, explains Thernstrom, may have been a higher regard for education among Jews compared to a greater interest among Irish and Italians in acquiring property and keeping the family unit together. The latter two groups may also have avoided the public school in favor of the more hospitable parochial school, which in turn "muted rather than heightened aspirations and fostered a sense of alienation from the larger society."[25] That hypothesis still requires careful testing, but Irish and Italian children during the late nineteenth and early twentieth centuries actually did complete fewer years of schooling, whether in public or parochial systems, and they were less mobile than Russian Jews.[26]

Despite indications that external factors weakened its possible effect, the public school eventually succeeded in attracting and holding the vast majority of school-age Americans. Statistics reported by the U.S. Office of Education revealed the dimensions of the victory: the proportion of children five to seventeen years of age enrolled in schools increased steadily from over 70 percent in 1900 to over 80 percent in 1930, and the proportion is continuing its upward climb.[27] Over the years, more children attended school regularly for ever-longer terms. In turn there is less illiteracy among black people, native whites, and foreign-born whites.[28] In addition, the data suggest positive correlations between job status, income, and years of schooling. By the early twentieth century, Timothy Smith was able to report that the social and economic aspirations of immigrants, especially Eastern and Southern Europeans, reflected the American attachment to schools. They might have resorted to parochial systems, but they were sending their children to school in increasing numbers.[29]

At the turn of the century, the successes were uneven, to be sure, and varied by ethnic group and location.[30] Italians followed different patterns in Boston than they did in Hartford. In large cities native whites and blacks tended to support school attendance more strongly than white ethnics. The children of Eastern and Southern European immigrants were more likely to be behind their age level in school than native white, German, or English counterparts.[31] And they attended class less regularly. Throughout the country, especially in urban centers with a heavy influx of recent immigrants, overcrowded schools turned children away—the Americanization imperative notwithstanding.[32]

Albert Fishlow argues that, even in regard to literacy, the success of the common school proved to be uneven at least during early stages of development.[33] Despite the claims of its antebellum advocates, the public school did not increase literacy, but, rather, built upon a preexistent American commitment to education evident in every section of the country. The school's major accomplishment, according to Fishlow, was in bringing education into the public sector rather than in making it available for new populations.

In regard to social mobility and job training, the school's effects may have been equally ambiguous. Samuel Bowles and Herbert Gintis insist that a student's social-class origins provide a more accurate prediction of job destination and income than years of schooling or academic achievement.[34] There is the additional possibility, suggested by Ivar Berg, that the positive correlation between years of schooling and job opportunity detectable in census data reflects a common practice of educationally upgrading positions even when the needed skills have little relation to those acquired through schooling.[35] To the extent that this occurs, schooling can hardly be credited as the direct cause of upward mobility.

It is fair to conclude that the public school has enjoyed mixed success in socializing American youth. Its roles have been limited and its effectiveness curtailed by other, sometimes more powerful, institutions and forces. Clearly, the school has not been the only, or even always the dominant, educational process available to the young. It is incapable, alone, of preparing them for adulthood. Furthermore, its effectiveness has been frequently undermined by patterns of exclusion and inequality reflecting both school policies and social practice. At best, the public school remains as a promise, however faulty in construction and incomplete in delivery, that the proper preparation of the young is a matter of public concern and commitment. Promises, of course, have little intrinsic value. This one only makes clear that proper preparation in terms of public policies and programs remains as a renewable assignment for future generations.

NOTES

1. *Connecticut Common School Journal* 1 (May 1839): 113.
2. Superintendent of Common Schools in Connecticut, *Eighth Annual Report* (1853), 180-182.
3. William T. Harris, "Elementary Education," in *Monographs on Education in the United States,* ed. Nicholas Murray Butler (Albany, N.Y.: J.B. Lyon Company, 1900).
4. *Ibid.,* 117.
5. *Ibid.,* 128-130.
6. See Donald R. Warren, *To Enforce Education: A History of the Founding Years of the United States Office of Education* (Detroit: Wayne State University Press, 1974), 98-107, 170-172.
7. See Michael B. Katz, *The Irony of Early School Reform: Educational Innovation in Mid-Nineteenth Century Massachusetts* (Cambridge, Mass.: Harvard University Press, 1968); Selwyn K. Troen, *The Public and the Schools: Shaping the St. Louis System, 1838-1920* (Columbia: University of Missouri Press, 1975).
8. Warren, *To Enforce Education,* 26-30.
9. Frank Winslow Johnson, "The Social Organization of the High School," *School Review* 17 (December 1909): 679.
10. *Ibid.,* 668.
11. Earle Rugg, "Special Types of Activities: Student Participation in Student Government," in *Extra-Curricular Activities,* Twenty-fifth Yearbook of the National Society for the Study of Education, Part II, ed. Guy M. Whipple (Bloomington, Ill.: Public School Publishing Co., 1926), 127-140.
12. Leonard V. Koos, "Analysis of the General Literature on Extra-Curricular Activities," *ibid.,* 1-22.
13. Herbert Croly, *The Promise of American Life* (Indianapolis, Ind.: Bobbs-Merrill Co., 1909), 400.
14. *Ibid.,* 407.
15. See Joel H. Spring, *Education and the Rise of the Corporate State* (Boston: Beacon Press, 1972), 13-21.
16. Quoted in Warren, *To Enforce Education,* 26.
17. *Ibid.,* 31.
18. Gregory Mason, "An Americanization Factory," *Outlook* 112 (February 23, 1916): 448.
19. Troen, *The Public and the Schools,* 55-78.
20. Jack M. Hall, *Juvenile Reform in the Progressive Era* (Ithaca, N.Y.: Cornell University Press, 1971), 309-316.
21. *Public Papers of the Presidents,* Volume I (Washington, D.C.: Government Printing Office, 1965), 413-414.
22. See Warren, *To Enforce Education,* 62-64, 195-196.
23. See, for example, Richard Sennett and Jonathan Cobb, *The Hidden Injuries of Class* (New York: Alfred A. Knopf, 1972).
24. Stephan Thernstrom, *The Other Bostonians: Poverty and Progress in the American Metropolis, 1880-1970* (Cambridge, Mass.: Harvard University Press, 1973), 222.
25. *Ibid.,* 174.
26. *Ibid.,* 170-175; see also Michael R. Olneck and Marvin Lazerson, "The School Achievement of Immigrant Children: 1900-1930," *History of Education Quarterly* 14 (Winter 1974): 453-482, reprinted in *History, Education, and Public Policy: Recover-*

ing the American Educational Past, ed. Donald R. Warren (Berkeley, Calif.: McCutchan Publishing Corp., 1978).

27. Reported in *Children and Youth in America: A Documentary History.* Volume II, *1866-1932,* Parts 7 and 8, ed. Robert H. Bremner (Cambridge, Mass.: Harvard University Press, 1971), 1101-1102.

28. *Ibid.,* 1103-1104.

29. Timothy L. Smith, "Immigrant Social Aspirations and American Education," *American Quarterly* 21 (Fall 1969): 523-543.

30. Olneck and Lazerson, "The School Achievement of Immigrant Children," 462-463.

31. See Leonard P. Ayres, *Laggards in Our Schools* (New York: Russell Sage Foundation, 1909), 103-116.

32. David B. Tyack, *The One Best System: A History of American Urban Education* (Cambridge, Mass.: Harvard University Press, 1974), 230-231.

33. Albert Fishlow, "The American Common School Revival: Fact or Fancy," in *Industrialization in Two Systems,* ed. Henry Rosovsky (New York: John Wiley and Sons, 1966), 40-67.

34. Samuel Bowles and Herbert Gintis, *Schooling in Capitalist America* (New York: Basic Books, 1976), 108-114.

35. See Ivar Berg, "Knowledge beyond Achievement: A Seventies Perspective on School Effects—A Review Symposium on the *Enduring Effects of Education,* by Herbert Hyman, Charles Wright, and John Reed," *School Review* 84 (February 1976): 283-289.

2. Smoothing the Way from School to Society

Harry S. Broudy

Our culture worships youthfulness, but is impatient with youth. Adults want the young to be thinking of the future, foreseeing consequences, practicing moderation in all things; to be respectful of the past and patient with the established order—in short, to exhibit the virtues of old age. The rate of human maturation satisfies no one. Everybody would like to exist forever in the prime of life, but, whereas previous ages have been content to philosophize about this ideal, ours has made it a matter of public policy, and implementing it has become a growth industry. The school, it is urged, should cooperate in the enterprise by smoothing and shortening the road from school to society.[1]

This chapter is concerned with some logical difficulties that beset controversies about the role of the school in preparing adolescents for nonschool life. These difficulties arise when parties to the debate appeal tacitly to principles and doctrines that explicitly they deny; when they invoke policies that, if implemented, would negate each other; when they propose changes in schools that ignore social reality. Although "foolish consistency" may be "the hobgoblin of little minds," chronic inconsistency is not a sign of educational statesmanship. It does not augur well for such statesmanship to have educators assert almost in the same breath such pairs of propositions as: The school is a disaster; dropping out of school is a disaster. The academic subject matter curriculum is an elitist oppression of the masses; real equality will come when the masses no longer have to study the elitist curriculum. Schooling is not related to social and economic life; lack of schooling is the cause of our social and economic ills. That Johnny or Jenny cannot read is a scandal; the trouble with the school is that it is too much concerned with words and concepts and not enough with feelings and personal relationships.

These statements, strictly speaking, may not be true contradictories, but asserting them in close conjunction and with equal zeal borders on incoherence. Incoherence takes its revenge when incompatible attitudes and beliefs are translated into school policy by school boards and school administrators. Much of the incoherence is the result of blurring several key distinctions in an understandable desire to have the school be all things to all of its clients. There is an example of this blurring of distinctions when each social institution has a special function for which it is primarily responsible and yet the community is organized so that every function is shared by all social agencies. Another example is the gap between knowledge as conceptualized in the academic disciplines and the use of knowledge in everyday life. Still another exists between the kind of schooling that all human beings need by virtue of being human and the specialized skills and knowledge needed for a vocation.

I shall not argue that these differences are absolute nor dispute the contention that they have a common origin in the efforts of man to master his environment. The persistence of the articulation problem does, however, indicate that they are more than verbal quibbles. There is something that prevents an easy translation of the formal disciplines into practical intelligence or technical skill, just as there is something about highly specialized technical skill and knowledge that does not enable it to meet all of the requirements of a good life.

I believe the key difference lies between a body of knowledge organized as a conceptual system (What is good chemistry?) and the use of such knowledge in solving concrete human problems (What is chemistry good for?). The logical gap between the criteria for the appropriate answers to these questions makes it difficult to pass from one to the other freely and strengthens the case for a special role for the secondary school; it also limits the kinds of study that could qualify as general education.

TWO VIEWS OF SOCIAL ORGANIZATION

In *The Republic* Plato argued that, in a rationally ordered society, the rearing of children, adjudicating domestic conflicts and carrying on foreign ones, and the production of goods and services would be carried on by special personnel and agencies. Government would be charged with orchestrating the efforts of all the other agencies in terms of the common good. Plato defended this mode of organization on the grounds that personnel devoted to a special task would carry it out more efficiently than a collection of jacks-of-all-trades doing all things indifferently.

Because human beings are served by many institutions, it is necessary to modify the principle of the division of labor so that each institution has a primary function for which it has the major responsibility and many ancillary functions by which it serves other institutions. For example, although instruction is entrusted to the school as its primary function, the theater, newspapers, and other agencies also provide information and shape attitudes as ancillary functions. This division of labor assumes that, because a function will be the prime concern of a particular institution, the failure or collapse of that institution will impair the performance of the function. Shifting of one function, therefore, necessitates adjustment in some or all of the others. Otherwise, there is a confusion of roles with an accompanying loss of efficiency. Accordingly, shifts and gross modification of function are not to be taken lightly and are often opposed because they threaten the social order.

This type of division of labor reflects a view of the cosmic order and indeed of being itself. Each item of reality has its proper end and function. Reality is organized in means-end chains that are rooted in the nature of things; they are not merely conventional. The rationale of these means-ends chains, Plato thought, might be glimpsed by the Guardians as a capstone to long practice in controlling their appetites and studying mathematics. Once in possession of the grand design, they could be trusted to legislate with wisdom and integrity without having to consult the will of the people.[2]

The opposite view of social organization holds that the roles and functions of social institutions are rooted in nothing more permanent than the needs of the group at a given time. As times and needs change, so do the functions that social institutions perform. Who does what is left to circumstance or negotiated by the various agencies.

There is much talk of cooperation and working together, so that the school, for example, is urged to work with parents, local industries, labor unions, welfare agencies, banks, the media, the utilities, and the environmentalists. Inasmuch as every institution serves everybody, there is no limit to the possible combinations of these working arrangements. Along with sharing the task, all institutions presumably share the responsibility as well.

The articulation problem sooner or later brings about a confrontation between these two views of social organization. The controversy, however, rarely finds the arguments in explicit opposition, and this is not surprising because there is enough difficulty and virtue in both views to prevent an unequivocal commitment to either.

In the absence of infallible Guardians to define and defend any fixed set of functions for the several social institutions and to orchestrate them for the common good, the highly specialized division of labor view can be legitimated only by an appeal to tradition, which begs the question so far as the opposition is concerned. Or one might appeal to experience to show that such societal specialization has in fact produced the good society. Unfortunately, examples that fulfill these conditions are hard to locate. Either the society was too simple or not good enough to prove the point at issue, or the principle was not applied with sufficient rigor, or, as was most often the case, strict divisions of labor have not been directed by wise and uncorrupted statesmen.

One could argue, of course, that in a democratic society the distribution of roles and functions should be decided by the will of the people, as are other matters of policy. This is feasible when a new agency (for example, Medicare or Social Security) is created, but the boundaries of established institutions were marked out long ago, and their personnel have vested interests in protecting them. Even if a plebiscite were the means by which a decision was made, the decision would be irrelevant, for a rational division of labor is grounded in rationality—in some intelligible design—and not in the wishes of any group. To justify the rationality of the democratic consensus, one must assume that the will of the majority is the voice of the Platonic Guardian.

Difficult as it is to defend a strict division of labor, once it is abandoned and all functions are then shared by all agencies, the difficulties are multiplied. There is no lack of variety in views about the actual and desirable roles of the police, the family, the church, the courts, and the media in education. There is no corporation or association with a public relations apparatus worthy of the name that is not anxious to share the school's burdens. They are only too glad to furnish materials that will enrich the curriculum and inculcate pupils with the proper values.

In schooling, as in other enterprises, once the sharing approach is adopted, proper allotment of responsibility becomes debatable, and recrimination among the sharers is the rule. Endless conferences are scheduled to provide a platform for these discussions, and they end with a call for all agencies to work together and to dedicate themselves to endless consultation with each other. Yet even this loose organization, strictly speaking, implies some discernible difference among the cooperating agencies based on some distinctive activity—a difference that is incompatible with the principle of indifference of function on which the sharing approach is based.

Schools have, however, been associated with knowledge in one sense or another too long to permit the literal application of the indifference of function principle. Even the most innovative and radical schools have books and chalkboards on the premises, and the most liberated of parents expect their children to know something as a result of going to school that they otherwise might not have learned. So whatever else the school may do to share in the work of the family, the industrial system, the law, and other social agencies, knowledge must be somewhere on its agenda. But where will it be in the school's ranking of priorities? The answer depends on how many noninstructional activities it undertakes and on its concept of knowledge. Most of the proposals for smoothing the road from school to adult life involve sampling life activities, many of which do not require study of a discipline. The justification for this move is that direct experience in the world of work and information about careers, for example, provides more useful forms of knowledge than academic subjects do, especially if academic learning "turns kids off." This brings us to a second set of distinctions, namely, those between knowledge as organized in the intellectual disciplines and task-oriented knowledge.

DISCIPLINARY KNOWLEDGE AND TASK-ORIENTED KNOWLEDGE

Knowledge, when refined and packaged by scholarship, is highly symbolic and abstract. The symbols are connected with their referents by convention. The word "cat" does not look like a cat; $2 + 2 = 4$ does not look like pairs of apples or people being converted into quartets. One has to be initiated into the conventions that give meaning to these symbols. Hence, schools or tutors are charged with letting the young in on the secrets of the symbolic systems. Johnny would not have to read if nobody wrote in nonpictorial language or even bothered to write at all.

The cleavage between conceptual systems and the ordinary activities of life is as old as the theoretical imagination. Although astronomy and mathematics may have had their origins in measuring and the building of pyramids, it took a radical leap of the human imagination to discern in those activities the nature of number and the laws of celestial motion—a leap credited to the curiosity of the Greeks. Some individuals, for a moment at least, had to forget action in order to capture the concept, that is, the idea that made understanding of the action possible. This leap from the existential to the theoretical mode has filled college catalogs with the results of scholarship, arcane theories, and esoteric information.

The history of pedagogy is replete with accounts of schoolmasters trying to cajole, persuade, or seduce the young into mastering the Latin language, geography, history, science, and other symbolic mysteries. Some educational reformers devoted themselves to schemes for embedding the studies in activities that naturally commanded children's interests; others proposed that the school abjure seduction altogether and become a place where young people lived rather than studied. Still others believed that, if only the pupil could recapitulate the history of the disciplines, the problem of motivation would be solved.

The chasm between the logical order of knowledge and the psychological order of learning remains, and examination of the literature of education will show that the same ploys for bridging the gap are still with us. The novel factor is the anomalous status of knowledge in a highly developed, technological, mass-production-oriented culture. On the one hand, it embodies the highest level of cognition, but, on the other, it does not demand that this knowledge or anything remotely resembling it be acquired by the consumer. In short, the system delivers the products of expertise to the nonexpert, and this is true for both ideational products and material ones; ready-made ideas and opinions are as available as precooked foods.

Is this delivery system sufficient to enlighten the public will? Is it sufficient for occupational, civic, and personal adequacy? One of the strangest oddities of our time is the simultaneous loss of credibility of economists, lawyers, physicians, politicians, and even accountants, on the one hand, and the increased use of these professionals, on the other. Their expertise cannot be picked up by the layman because much of that expertise is grounded in disciplinary knowledge. It is useless to exhort the citizen to think for himself—as his yeoman ancestors were supposed to do in a free society—if he does not have the concepts or the skills to gather and process the data that would allow him to think for himself. There are few strictly local issues left. Congressional committees have to hire experts in order to carry on their investigations—moral indignation is not enough.[3]

The transition from adolescence to adulthood, from school to life, hinges on our analysis of this situation. The proposals to incorporate experiments in community life, apprentice training on jobs, enrollment in service agencies, in short, quasi-real encounters with the real world no doubt will ameliorate many of the current discontents that adolescents experience in high school. Turning the school into an adjustatorium[4] may lower the crime rate, drug addiction, and VD among the young. But none of these measures does precisely what study of formalized subject matter is supposed to do. How much of the school's efforts shall go into such study, and how much of it should be prescribed for all or part of the school population? These questions cannot be evaded indefinitely. Failing to make the distinction between the mastery of disciplinary knowledge and the activities of everyday life encourages the evasion.

The arguments for prescribing disciplinary studies at the secondary level are far from compelling. First, they are not needed to get or to hold many jobs that require limited skills. Second, mass production and modern technology make goods and services available to many persons who have little formal schooling. Third, through adult and continuing education, those who, for one reason or another, want a second chance for formal study can have it. But these arguments, persuasive though they are, misconstrue the way disciplinary studies operate in society and in the life of the individual. Their effects are never direct, and the attempt to hitch every effect to a school episode is futile.

If the school has any impact on society as a whole, it is as a preprofessional training ground in the disciplines. Aside from this, it has some influence on the modes of thought and feeling of those who have undergone a fairly extensive exposure to general education. Holders of the bachelor's degree should have acquired the categories of the major disciplines. Whether or not they can be recalled in adult life, they function tacitly in providing the contexts within which particular situations of life are rendered intelligible. Many a college graduate cannot pass a college examination in economics, but he will construe economic events differently from those who never studied economics. And the same may be claimed for the study of the sciences and the arts, whether in high school or in college. A population disciplined by the disciplines would have a considerable and important effect on the social order, but it would be indirect. One would be hard put to trace the effects of each college or high school course on adult life. To those who understand how general education functions, it would be misguided to attempt such tracing in the first place.

It must be concluded, therefore, that the retention of the traditional or academic curriculum in the secondary school is justified for those who plan to go to college, or who may need certain subjects such as mathematics or some of the sciences in vocational curricula. It is also justified for those who place some value on the kind of general education that study of the disciplines makes possible. For all others such schooling is a matter of choice and taste.

Proponents of the nonacademic curriculum might, however, take exception to the role of the academic disciplines in general education. The academic curriculum is general in that the disciplines are highly generalizable, inasmuch as they constitute the most universal forms of thought we have. But there can be another meaning to general education, namely, proficiency in a sample of the tasks most frequently encountered in ordinary life. Driving an automobile, filling out an income tax form, reading directions, fixing a water faucet, and voting are just a few of the tasks that would be on the list. Participating in a wide variety of community activities also belongs to this kind of general education; one can gain a valuable familiarity with the culture by participating in its institutions.

Which of these types of general education, if any, will prove more beneficial to most people in the kind of society that might exist twenty-five years from now is hard to predict, but each shapes the mind in different ways. Disciplinary study makes much higher cognitive demands than learning by doing and participating in real life activities. Those who enjoy theoretical activity for its own sake are biased in its favor and find it difficult to imagine anyone feeling otherwise. The European tradition separated the elites from the masses by early streaming into the *Gymnasium* or the *Volksschule,* as in Germany. Encouraging our young people to make the same sort of choice early in life would have the same effect, and justifying it on the grounds of democratic egalitarianism is a strange and subtle sort of fraud. On the contrary, nothing will push us further and faster toward restoring the notion that theoretical and humane studies are for the classes and that vocational training and social docility will do for the masses.

THE SCHOOL AND SOCIETY AS SOCIAL REALITIES

The charge that the traditional academic-oriented high school is out of gear with reality is well founded. It is out of gear in two ways: first, there is the gap between the structure of knowledge and that of ordinary life; second, the traditional school stands *in loco communitatis, parentis,* and *humanitatis* in their ideal, not actual, form. A teacher of social studies knows that any attempt to portray the community as it is would rouse the indignation of the public in general and of politicians in particular. This should be kept in mind when schemes for tearing down the walls between school and community are proposed.

The school performs many functions that may have little to do with instruction. For example, because schools bring together large numbers of pupils, it is convenient to have their eyes, ears, and teeth examined in school. Furthermore, if the community fails to provide the conditions necessary for instruction—proper nutrition, emotional security, bilingual instruction, physical safety—the school may have to provide them.

We look to the school to perform a supervisory function that at one time was largely the responsibility of the family, the neighborhood, and, on occasion, the police. Today community supervision of the young seldom exists; working parents are often forced to entrust their children to a custodial agency for many hours of the day. And the mobility of adolescents via the automobile makes it difficult, if not impossible, to monitor their movements if they choose to conceal them.

The school serves as a social yardstick for individual development. Age and grade roughly constitute the measure, so that uninterrupted progress through the grades is of more interest to the public than what goes on in the grades.

The school is a loosely organized but genuine adolescent community. It is the place where most adolescents are and do what adolescents like to do. Study is for many young people incidental to attending school. The ability of the school to manifest, reinforce, and inculcate the values of the community is in direct proportion to the homogeneity of the values held by its constituents. The simultaneous demand that schools teach values and allow for the development of cultural pluralism is another of the incoherences endemic to educational literature. If the school celebrates in song and story and by precept and example the virtues of the middle class, it cannot be wholehearted in celebrating the values of sexual permissiveness, unconfined and unrefined hedonism, and ripping off the establishment. Only if the school is allowed to stand as a representative of a cultural tradition that transcends biases of classes and cultures can it be effective as an exemplar of values. The ability of the school to engage in value education or character education or civic education depends on the reinforcement supplied by community models. The credibility of such models, we are told, is at all-time low.

Furthermore, societies or subsocieties that effectively socialize the young utilize a wide variety of rites to impress upon the individual the importance of the passage into adulthood. Scarification, temporary isolation, and ordeals of all sorts mark these rites. Even the study of the Latin language has been regarded as a puberty rite.[5] The absence of such rites in both the community and the school testifies to the lack of homogeneity within the value systems of the culture. Even access to the privilege of voting goes uncelebrated save for the act of registration. Naturalized citizens do go through a ceremony of sorts, perhaps because the right to vote is more important to them than to those who acquire it by birth. Rites and ceremonies do not cause social solidarity, but they do demonstrate it.

In support of these observations, one might point to the fact that some schools have served as effective maturation vats for the young and thus eased their transition to adult life. Private secondary schools, military schools, and religious schools often do precisely what the public secondary school is now asked to do, but without the benefit of a homogeneous, supportive clientele.

College sororities and fraternities have provided specialized socialization on college campuses that draw students from a wide spectrum of social classes and life-styles. The American liberal arts college has claimed to build character and to serve as a maturing vat, as well as being a site for higher learning. This claim is heard less often nowadays because, since the 1960s "good" colleges have hired staff to whom scholarship ranked above character training or socialization.

Finally, any real change in the function of the public schools requires a lead time of about an educational generation. Teachers, textbooks, styles of teaching, and school governance change very slowly, because to change the "system" means altering the perceptions and attitudes of more than 40 million pupils and more than 2.5 million teachers at about the same time. Is it any wonder that the expensive innovations of a decade or more largely disappeared when the stimulating grants ceased?[6]

I have argued, first, that a clear distinction can be drawn between disciplinary studies and learning by direct or quasi-direct participation in life activities, and, second, that if the American secondary school is to have a special function, it is to induct adolescents into the modes of thought and feeling exemplified by the disciplines. This function, it seems to me, is not likely to be performed by any other agency, nor will it accrue as a by-product of social participation.

I have tried to suggest that whether pupils avail themselves of this kind of study must be left to the students themselves or to their appointed guardians. The peculiar conditions and demands of modern technological societies provide arguments both for and against choosing it. No obviously dire penalties threaten the individual who does not choose it, but there is little hope that a technologically sophisticated, mass-production-oriented society can survive as a democracy unless the majority of the electorate does choose to become generally educated.

The use of the secondary school years for general education in the disciplinary mode may not be as ridiculous and reactionary as many educational reformers would have us believe if twenty-five years hence the labor market were to have no use for young people under the age of eighteen; if leisure, once the privilege of the very privileged classes, weighs as heavily on the young as it now does on the aged; and if a satisfactory life comes to depend upon the resources of an educated mind.[7]

The leisure class is no longer made up of elitist professionals—for whom their work is everything—but of workers employed at more or less routine jobs—for whom the job is the least likely source of satisfaction but which provides large amounts of leisure. Frenetic searches for identity, freedom, selfhood, serenity—now being exploited by innumerable cults, astrologers, liberationists, and others—might be more easily controlled by the educated mind.

The school can be made to do and be whatever its constituents wish. In the shifting of functions it would be a pity if the inducting of the young into the cultivation of the mind were lost in the shuffle or sequestered in private schools or available only to a small portion of the population attending public schools.

An even more serious loss would be to deprive the school as an institution of any claim to autonomy. For about the only way it can legitimate its claim to decide on matters of curriculum, methods of teaching, and educational policy in general is to appeal to the authority of scholars within the disciplines. However feeble the defense for this authority is philosophically, it is the only viable authority in terms of the social reality. Without such autonomy and authority, it is almost meaningless to speak of responsibility in the social order.

NOTES

1. The wisdom literature on these themes is voluminous; reflections on the stages of man and their respective rewards and infirmities have been favorite themes for essayists. The characteristics of each stage of life are remarkably constant. Aristotle's description, for example, would fit rather well as a special article in the Sunday supplement of our more literate newspapers. See *Rhetoric,* $1389^{a}2$-$1390^{b}11$.

2. No one realized better than Plato how outrageous his scheme for the ideal state was. The proposals that the Guardians be deprived of private families and fortunes were topped only by the even more radical notion that the Guardians should be philosopher-kings. These proposals have provoked social theorists in every age to prove that Plato was wrong and that private families, private fortunes, and nonphilosophical Guardians were compatible with a good, if not a perfect, society. The efforts to refute the Platonic outrages by sensible compromises show little signs of abatement or success.

3. Ralph Nader's attempt to combine research with indignation gains credibility as much from his reputed asceticism as from the quality of his research. His research is believed by consumers who have not the slightest notion of how valid it is. The trust is grounded not in the criteria of scientific evidence but in the apparent fact that Nader has no private axe to grind.

4. Back in 1954 I wrote in *Building a Philosophy of Education* (Englewood Cliffs, N.J.: Prentice-Hall, 1954, 1961) about establishing an adjustatorium as an alternative to the secondary school. At the time I was only half-serious about it, but many correspondents took it altogether seriously and wanted to know how, when, and where they could visit one. Today the notion seems a bit less odd than in the 1950s, because so many of the reforms of the high school seem to be envisioning something like it. I had suggested that adolescents need a period in which to straighten out their emotional and social maladjustments, and that the adjustatorium would be staffed with counselors of all kinds rather than teachers. Much of what since has come to be called the search for identity, consciousness raising, adjustment to one's feelings would have fitted into the activities of the adjustatorium. Today these activities are being suggested as part of the standard high school curriculum on the ground that the young need and want them. This may be so, but it does not follow therefrom that the needs have to be met in the high school.

5. Walter J. Ong, "Latin Language Study as a Renaissance Puberty Rite," *Studies in Philology* 56 (April 1959): 103-104.

6. For a helpful summary of the diverse studies and proposals in this field, see A. Harry Passow, "Once Again: Reforming Secondary Education," *Teachers College Record* 77 (December 1975): 161-188.

7. Professor B. E. Anderson of the Wharton School is quoted as saying that the teenage job gap will not be closed even by the fullest measure of full employment. *New York Times,* February 15, 1976, E4.

3. The Ways of Socialization

James S. Coleman

One of the principal tasks of any society is the socialization of its young. Until very recently, the major portion of these socialization functions [was] carried out within the family, a condition which, by its very informal and natural character, obscured the variety of these functions and the processes through which they occurred.

But as the family has shrunk in size and function, more of socialization has taken place outside it and in social structures unrelated to it, such as the school and the peer group. This change provides both an opportunity and a need for sociological analysis. The opportunity arises because the processes are less hidden within the confines of the family; the need because, in the family's default, responsibility arises at a broader social level, and social structures must be consciously constructed to carry out these functions if socialization of youth is to be more than a haphazard process.

Many issues arise once the socialization task becomes an obligation of the society-at-large and not merely of the child's immediate and extended family. Some of these have arisen in education, for schools were the first major institutions in which society took both authority and responsibility from the family for a set of socialization tasks. I will not address the general issues here, but will examine one issue only, a question that has received less attention than it deserves, both from

---

Reprinted, with permission, from *The Center Magazine* 9 (May-June 1976): 3-10.

those concerned with the practice of youth socialization and those concerned with its theory. This is the question of the quality and quantity of relations between a young person and others different in age.

For purposes of the present examination, I will mean by "young person" anyone older than about ten years who is still in school full time and unmarried. Thus the age range is about ten to twenty, though for many the period ends before twenty, and for some it extends beyond twenty. The questions I want to ask about young persons of this age can be asked for persons of any age in society; the answers provide important information about the structure of society. But the answers for this age range and for younger children tell also about the social structure within which new generations are initiated into society.

Perhaps the reason for neglect of these questions lies in the fact that the most intimate, most pervasive, and mose important organization in nearly all societies has been an age-heterogeneous organization, the family. Only as the family shrivels and some of its functions are replaced by age-homogeneous organizations does the question of age in relation to social structure become an important one.

In setting out to study age-structuring in socialization, several kinds of questions are important. [The first] is a merely descriptive one: What are the typical patterns both today and at various points in the past? Part of this question is quantitative: How much time, engaged in what activities, do young persons spend with persons not their own age, and what is the structural form of the relation? Part is qualitative: What is the nature of each of these relations? Authoritative? Exploitative? Collegial? Permissive? Personal? Impersonal? Intimate? How long-term? Frequency of contact?

After these descriptive questions, the immediate questions to follow are causal ones: What is the socialization effect of each of these patterns? That is, what is learned in each of these structures? What is learned, of course, depends not only on the intentions of the older persons, nor only on the intentions of the younger ones; there is also incidental learning which takes place without conscious intention by either. Many persons cannot say, for example, how they came to want to begin smoking. The answerability of the causal questions lies in the fact that at any time in society, a wide variety of socialization patterns exists, and careful study can allow inferences about the differing consequences of different patterns.

Finally, following the causal questions come normative ones. What should the patterns be? The normative questions cannot be completely answered by recourse to empirical fact as can the descriptive and causal questions, but empirical facts which answer the causal questions can narrow the normative questions to irreducible issues about what kinds of persons the society should produce.

It is common to say that academic disciplines—at least those other than moral philosophy and ethics—should steer as far from normative questions as possible. However, I think the matter is quite the reverse in this case: we should come as close as possible to the normative questions, to inform the political process by which they must be ultimately resolved. For those normative questions are in fact resolved by the very socialization structures that are established in society, and it is these socialization structures that determine what society's next generation will be like. As long as the normative questions were largely resolved in the family with primary consequences for its children alone, they could safely be ignored. But that is no longer the case.

A single example will indicate just how the social structure within which youth socialization takes place affects the content and the outcomes of that socialization. After the Second World War, there was a baby boom, beginning about 1946 and continuing into the 1950s. The direct consequence of this is that there were many more persons in their teens in 1965, and in their twenties in 1975, than there were a decade earlier. The indirect consequences of this bulge was a disproportion of youth to adults beginning in the early 1960s, when the advancing wave of the population bulge was in its early teens, and continuing to the present. Only in the 1970s has this first wave of the bulge moved into young adulthood.

This increase in the ratio of youth to adults in the 1960s was not merely a change in relative numbers. It was a disproportion between the size of the youth cohorts and the capacity of the socialization institutions, both the formal ones like schools and colleges, and less formal ones such as adult-led youth groups. There were shortages of teachers, of classrooms, of schools and colleges, of youth groups such as church-sponsored groups and scouts. Altogether, there was a shortage of adults for the socialization of youth. As a consequence, there grew up in the 1960s many forms of peer socialization, as well as ideologies exalting freedom from adults: free schools, communes, spontaneous youth groups such as radical political groups and religious groups, drug cultures which spurned adult mores concerning drug use, the rock music culture, and other manifestations.

It is not possible to know to what extent these developments among youth in the 1960s can be attributed to the relative numbers of youth and adults; some of the developments are more directly traceable to numbers than others. But it is clear that the sharp change in relative numbers of youth and adults was an important factor in the "youth phenomena" of the 1960s.

This change in relative numbers, and the incapacity of socializing institutions in the face of the increase in numbers of youth, changed the very structural forms through which socialization of youth took place. Because of the scarcity of adults, the number of direct personal relations with adults declined for the average young person, and a larger fraction of the contact between youth and adults was through an intermediary, the mass media of newspapers and television. This change in socialization structures, together with the consequences it had for the outcomes of socialization, suggests the importance of a careful examination of the specific structural forms through which youth are socialized.

It is the outlines of such an examination that I want to sketch here. In contrast to the usual focus on the content and intent of socialization, I want to focus attention on its structural form. In particular, I will discuss five such structures:

One-to-one socialization, involving one adult and one young person
One-to-many
Three-actor structures
Self-socialization structures among youth themselves
Mass media socialization

In each case, I will describe the most salient aspects of the structure, suggest some of its possible consequences, and raise the questions to which answers are necessary if the normative questions of how youth should be socialized are to be knowledgeably addressed.

ONE-TO-ONE SOCIALIZATION STRUCTURES

The classical conception of the socialization process is the simplest structure of all: one adult and one young person. The educational setting often regarded as the ideal is that of one adult and one young person, expressed by the phrase, "Mark Hopkins on a log." Yet this socialization structure is less frequent in practice than in discussion. It seldom exists in schools, and is probably most extensive in the home, between parent and child. It is obviously important there, as it is outside the home in noninstitutional settings. It was once prominent in the institution of apprenticeship, and still functions in a few craft and professional settings.

There are two important kinds of questions about one-to-one socialization of a child by an adult. One concerns the internal processes: the question of how socialization occurs, how it depends on the nature of the relation between the two persons, and how this in turn depends upon the behavior of the adult. Theories, research, and practical handbooks of child rearing address themselves to these questions, and I shall have nothing to add here—except to note that in most such work, the one-to-one socialization structure is assumed, with little attention given to other structures, indeed, often with the implicit assumption that the same principles hold in other socialization structures. Much that is written concerning teaching or pedagogy makes this assumption as well, despite the fact that the teacher ordinarily is in a one-to-many structure.

The second kind of question to ask about one-to-one socialization structures concerns their incidence as a function of the social structure itself. How often is a young person in contact with an adult in a one-to-one structure, in a relation strong and continuous enough that some socialization takes place? As the everyday activities of typical family life change, the incidence of such settings between parent and child change. As the divorce rate goes up, this incidence goes down. As the extended family declines, the frequency of close relations to an adult other than the parent goes down. As more work comes to be carried out in organizational settings removed from children and youth, the incidence of these one-to-one relations decreases. As young persons spend more time in school, where there are seldom one-to-one socialization settings, the opportunity for such relations declines.

In order to know just what the potential is for socialization through one-to-one relations between an adult and a young person, extensive work in the ecology of youth and adults is necessary. Roger Barker and his associates in ecological psychology have begun this work and have provided a methodology for such research. When the results of extensive research in this direction are in, the basis will exist for the design of institutional structures that open up opportunities for fruitful one-to-one socialization of youth by adults.

I say "fruitful" because it is of course not true that all relations between an adult and a young person are beneficial to the latter. Indeed, our institutional isolation of youth from personal relations with adults is a result of the conception of a brutalizing adult society outside the home and outside the school from which children and youth must be protected. The protection remains necessary, but the brutalizing and corrupting character of adults for youth other than their own children may have decreased as civilization and education have increased, while the insulation between individual youth and individual adults has grown thicker. This, of course, means that a higher proportion of the total socialization of youth takes place in other structures.

It would not be correct to prejudge the question of what socialization structures are "best." What is necessary, however, is to know how the overall institutional structure of society affects the incidence of various structures through which socialization takes place. Although it appears evident that various institutional changes have reduced the incidence of one-to-one socialization of youth, our present knowledge tells us little more about the specific factors that affect this incidence.

ONE-TO-MANY SOCIALIZATION STRUCTURES

A large amount of the socialization that young persons undergo is carried out in a structure with one adult and a large number of young persons as learners. The most evident role relationship in this case is that of teacher and students, as in a typical classroom. But this is not the only form. Another is that of coach and team, a relationship that exhibits very different characteristics. Still others, closer to coach than to teacher, are bandleader and band, or play director and cast of actors. A relationship that ordinarily goes under the heading of teacher-student, but is clearly different, is that of laboratory instructor supervising a number of laboratory groups.

The simplest structure is the usual classroom structure, in which the only recognized or legitimate relationship is between the teacher and each student, or the teacher and the class as an unstructured aggregate of students. In actual classrooms, there are often variations upon this, with some students having specialized roles, such as recording absences, and the relation that exists between teacher and student differs somewhat for different students. Yet there are many classrooms which approximate the ideal type.

The kinds of socialization for which this classroom structure appears most appropriate are those involving transmission of information from teacher to students. This is the intended classical function of the school, and thus it is not surprising that schools exhibit largely this form.

Certain questions that arise with this structure are evident from its very form. Since it does not recognize and provide a function for student-student relations, yet tends to generate such relations, one important question concerns these relations: How do they affect the relation between teacher and students? For example, the prestige or status structure among students in a classroom can greatly affect the learning that takes place: if the high-status students are uninterested in learning what the teacher has to transmit, others will become uninterested, too. Or a second example: the relations among students can generate great disorder in a classroom, making difficult any disciplinary control. If a teacher recognizes these relations among students, the very relations themselves can sometimes be used to restore or maintain order.

However, despite these obvious examples of the importance of social structure among the students, the prevailing beliefs about the teacher's function are blind to the structure. These beliefs stem from the ideal of a two-person, one-to-one socialization structure: one teacher and one student. The beliefs emphasize the importance of "individual attention," of "treating each student as an individual," and totally ignore the social structure among students. The naivete of these beliefs has probably been as responsible as any other single factor for the unpreparedness of new teachers faced with a classroom of junior high or high school students.

More research has been done on this structure—the one-to-many classroom structure—than on any other structure of socialization. The work has been done under the headings of sociometry in the classroom, social climates in schools, adolescent subcultures in school, classroom observation, and the like. Publications have included both sociological analyses and firsthand accounts by quondam teachers. The amount of information, in one place and another, about this structure is probably sufficiently great to warrant a review and synthesis that would inform the socialization process. Such a synthesis could begin to answer the following questions: What kind of orientation can a teacher best take toward the social organization of the students, as distinct from his orientation toward the individual students? How does the relation between teacher and class affect the social organization of the class, and what is the reverse effect? How do the social organization and the informal culture among students affect learning? For what socialization functions is a class of students best treated as an unstructured aggregate, and for what functions is it best to use or even generate structure among the students? What are the socialization consequences of different kinds of social structures generated in a class?

Turning to one-to-many structures other than that of teacher and an aggregate of students, probably the most common is that of coach and team.* A coach's function is much different than that of a teacher, whether he is coach of a football team or a debate team. He is not the center of attention, as a classroom teacher ordinarily is, but is on the sidelines, while the young [team members'] attention is directed to the activities they are engaged in. He provides evaluation, criticism, direction, advice, all designed to increase the performance level of the team—and as a by-product, that of its members.† Curiously, although he is on the sidelines, while the teacher is at the students' center of attention, for the young person exposed to both, he is often far more important for incidental socialization functions than is the teacher. In common parlance, he makes a greater impression upon the young people he coaches than do most teachers on the young persons they teach.

Perhaps the central definitional difference between the role of the coach and that of the teacher is that the teacher is concerned with [the] individual performance of each student in a class, while the coach is concerned with the collective or team performance.‡ As a consequence, a major part of the coach's activity is creating relationships among the members: making a team out of an aggregate of

*In this category can be also located band director and band, or drama director and cast of actors, although the role relationships differ slightly from that of coach and team. Like the coach and unlike the teacher, the band director and the drama director (who is also often called a coach) are concerned with performance of an organized collectivity, not individual performance.

†Some coaches, who see their goal more as training young persons than as winning, reverse the above goals, so that the primary goal is increasing the young persons' performance levels, the performance level of the team being a by-product.

‡This is also true, of course, for the coach in an individual sport, such as track, for although the activities are individual, the goal is collective. One consequence, for example, is that only the best performers in any event compete, and the poor performers merely drop out.

young persons. The existence of the collective goal strengthens and develops this structure of relations among team members, so that the resulting socialization structure is at the polar extreme from that of the aggregate classroom.

Research and other writing on socialization within such a structure is less abundant than that on the teacher-classroom structure. It consists largely of popular accounts of coaches, or coaches and teams, with only a few sociological studies emerging in a developing field of the sociology of sport. So, we are only at the beginning of systematic knowledge about socialization within the coach-team structure.

It is useful to note here that some structures which begin as one-to-many are transformed into a three-actor structure by the adult. Adult-sponsored or adult-led youth clubs as discussed earlier are like this. Through establishing one or more young people as leader or authority, the adult moves to the role of supervisor, shaping the behavior of the young person in authority toward those in the group.

THREE-ACTOR SOCIALIZATION STRUCTURES

Some socialization activities involve three ages, rather than two. Perhaps the best example is child-rearing practice. To a great extent in an extended family, and to some extent in a modern family, young persons, especially girls, learn about raising children through a structure involving themselves, their mother, and a younger child or infant in the family. A daughter takes care of the child, and the mother provides instruction. The general paradigm involves the older person as instructor or supervisor, the young person as actor, and the still younger person (that is, the infant) as object of the young person's activity.

Such a structure appears widespread, at least for learning about child rearing. Beatrice Whiting, in her study of child rearing in six primitive cultures in Africa, finds a pattern as follows: a boy or girl aged about five to nine will be placed in charge of a younger child (at least two years younger) while the mother is at work, for example, in the field. The five-to-nine-year-old learns many of the activities of care for the young in this way, depending on the mother for the necessary instruction, but learning through actual responsibility for care of the younger child.

Such a paradigm would appear applicable wherever the task to be learned by the young person is care of dependent persons. In hospital settings, for example, young girls, working as volunteers, learn about care of the sick under the supervision of professionals older than they are. Young girls working in nursery schools exemplify the same paradigm, learning to take care of nursery-age children under the supervision of an older woman.

But there are other situations, also quite frequent, that fit the paradigm. Boy and girl scouts are examples. In scouting, an adult scout leader is in overall charge. But there are other leaders who are young persons, only a few years older than the youngest scouts: junior assistant scoutmaster, senior patrol leader, patrol leader. In this structure, the young persons in leadership positions are, as in the child-rearing case, engaged in responsibilities involving others—and thus learning how to carry out such responsibility—under the supervision of someone older than themselves.

In schools, this pattern sometimes exists as well, most often in extracurricular clubs and activities: a teacher serves as the supervisor or sponsor, but the young persons who are the club or activity leaders are the ones engaged in directing and managing others. Practice teaching is another example: a young person engages in classroom teaching, under the supervision of an adult leader, learning to manage a classroom and teach children through helping an adult teacher do so, and through actual practice under the eyes of the adult teacher.

This second class of situations which fit the three-person paradigm, from scouting to practice teaching, constitutes an important class. It appears to be useful for learning to function in an authority structure. The classic case is that of British boys' boarding schools, the "public schools," in which authority is largely exercised by older boys over the younger boys, under the supervision of the adult masters. This structure appears to have been almost ideally designed to provide the socialization necessary for administrators in the British Empire. The excesses of this system, primarily involving sadistic practices on the part of the older boys, serve as a reminder that results can vary widely and that the fine structure of the relations is important to their functioning, just as in two-person socialization structures.

It is clear that the three-person paradigm is an important one for socialization. Yet we know little about it in general. What is the principal function of the older person:

As a *role model,* whose activities are imitated by the younger, who is learning? If so, the critical qualification for the older person is his own behavior when he has authority over others or responsibility for them.

As an *instructor,* whose principal function is to instruct and criticize the younger in his performance? If so, his more important qualities are his understanding of and insight into the authority or responsibility or care as another person exercises it, and his ability to communicate this.

As a *standard setter* or *goal setter,* whose principal function is to establish the criteria or standards that the learner should meet? If so, his most important qualities may be his sense of when to be rigid, when to be yielding, and how demanding he can be before the negative consequences outweigh the positive ones.

We also know little about the effects of the relation between the older person and the younger or the younger's behavior toward the dependent person. What is the effect of the level of intimacy, or the hierarchical distance? How does the attitude of the younger toward the older affect his behavior and thus his learning, and what influences those attitudes?

Finally, no one has engaged in a cataloging of the kinds of skills that are typically learned in three-person structures. In the preceding comments, I have mentioned care of children, care of other dependent persons, and exercise of administrative authority in a hierarchy. But this is only a beginning.

The study of three-person socialization structures has a special importance, because not all social structures provide natural settings in which an adult, a young person, and a younger or a dependent person are simultaneously found. Particularly with the age segregation of modern society, such settings do not naturally occur with high frequency. Thus unless there are purposive attempts to establish such structures, these socialization functions may be poorly carried out. In many parts of modern society, I suspect these structures have not been established, and the socialization which ordinarily takes place within them is missing. I will mention two examples only. As a first example—most severe for middle-class youth—the smaller-size families and [narrower] age range of children within the family reduce the child care that a young person can carry out under the general supervision of a parent, preventing his learning of the activities of a parent. A second example—most severe for lower-class youth—is the undersupply of, and variable quality of, volunteer adult leaders for youth groups such as scouts and other groups. Our social structure does not generate an adequate supply of such adult volunteers, and in their absence young people are denied important aspects of socialization, the exercise of authority and leadership.

MANY-ACTOR SELF-SOCIALIZATION STRUCTURES

This is another very important socialization structure that I must mention, though my attention in this article is directed to the relation of youth and adults. This is self-socialization among the young themselves, in play groups or in games. Jean Piaget has shown in fine detail how simple games such as marbles function to develop conceptions of a moral order: conceptions of rules, of laws, of constitutional agreements. Others have described and cataloged the variety of games that children play in the streets and playgrounds.

Although I will not dwell on this pattern of self-socialization of the young through play and games, it is necessary to point out that children live in worlds created by adults. The social and institutional settings that adults provide for them—either purposively, as in a school, or unintentionally, as in the construction of a high-rise apartment building that has no meeting places for the young—affect greatly the development of self-socialization structures among youth and what is learned within them. For example, schools as constituted create single-year age groups through their grade structure, with some isolation between the single-year groups, and greater isolation between groups three or four years in age span (that is, junior high school, senior high school, college). What consequence does this have for the trickle-down learning that occurs from one age to another a year or two below it? Even casual knowledge of schools and colleges tells us that there are many attitudes, actions, and items of information for which the chasm between junior and senior high school, and between high school and college, is an effective barrier to the trickle-down process of socialization. Indeed, part of the reason for the separation of these age groups, particularly in creation of the junior high school, was just this, to insulate the young from "corruption" by those a few years older. But beneficial as well as corrupting things are learned along these age chains, and thus it is important to know better than we do now the consequences of particular forms of institutional insulation between ages.

These consequences are not, of course, independent of the surrounding social structure. On the one hand, when the family was a larger and more age-heterogeneous unit, the school's age insulation mattered less because sibling relations bridged that insulation. On the other hand, the increased importance of television's vicarious experiences reduces the age insulation for learning certain kinds of things, perhaps especially those conceived as "corrupting," though not for learning other things.

In order to design appropriate institutions in the presence of self-socialization and trickle-down socialization processes of youth, detailed knowledge of what is learned through these processes, of the sort that Piaget provides for younger children, is necessary. Also necessary is detailed knowledge of the effect of institutional structures, such as age grading in school, on these processes of socialization that occur among youth themselves.

The central point is that socialization in modern society is increasingly dependent upon consciously established institutional structures, as the multimember and multifunction family disappears. The incidental and spontaneous structures of socialization that develop in and around these institutions are no less important than the formally created ones.

MASS MEDIA SOCIALIZATION

The most modern structure of socialization, and the one about which the least is known, is that which takes place through the mass media. Books, ranging from textbooks to novels, have long been a primary mass medium of socialization. Television is now the most prominent medium through which socialization occurs, and its range is equally great—from "Sesame Street" and the Open University for teaching cognitive skills and knowledge to dramas in which violence is vividly exhibited.

Again, two kinds of questions are important to ask about this form of socialization. [The first] is the question of the processes themselves: What is learned? And how is it learned? What is learned by children who watch "Sesame Street" or the "Electric Company," or youth who watch programs in the Open University? What is the effect on children of violence on television? How do the implicit moral standards expressed in television shows affect the development of moral judgment in children and youth?

The second [kind of] question again concerns the incidence of socialization through television. The questions here concern not only who watches what, and at what ages, but also . . . the other socialization structures to which these children and youth are subject. For the importance of television as a socialization agent depends on the presence or absence of other structures, which, if absent, leave a vacuum and, if present, make television less important. It appears probable that television's primary impact is not in competition with the stronger personal socialization processes, but in their absence. Thus, to learn the incidence of socialization through television it is important to know the incidence of socialization through the interpersonal processes discussed earlier.

4. The School and the Acquisition of Values

Jacob W. Getzels

The central issue facing the schools today, as always, is the problem of values. For, whether we will it or not—indeed, whether we know it or not—the choices educators or parents make regarding educational goals, content of curriculum, methods of instruction, even the shape of the classrooms we construct, are based on *some* system of values, however subconsciously they may be held in any particular case. Whatever else the child may be expected to do, or actually does, in school he is inevitably exposed, explicitly or implicitly, to these values.

I would like to direct attention to two related questions: First, what is the character of dominant American values and what are the shifts and cleavages in these values as they impinge upon the school? Second, what is the effect of these shifts and cleavages on the education of our children, and especially on the nature of the values they acquire?

I repeat here a number of observations from papers written in the 1950s and 1960s. Such repetition is unavoidable since consideration of the prevailing condition is not possible without reference to preceding conditions.[1]

NATIONAL SACRED VALUES

There are almost as many definitions of value as there are of personality or of culture. The definition I am using is borrowed from Clyde Kluckhohn: "A value is a conception, explicit or implicit, distinctive of an individual or characteristic of a group, of the *desirable* which influences the selection from available modes, means, and ends of action."[2]

As one looks at Americans from this point of view, we seem in many ways an enigma. At one time our values appear obvious and clear cut; at another time they seem elusive and complicated in the extreme.[3] The American foreground is full of contrasts and similarities, of obvious continuities and egregious discontinuities, of North and South, black and white, rich and poor, young and old. Where do our values overlap? Where do they diverge?

Our values overlap at the ideological level in the American creed. For there is an American creed, as Myrdal pointed out in *An American Dilemma,* which has been variously enunciated since Jefferson first wrote it.[4] The creed sets forth our basic and undivorceable beliefs. In Charles Morris's terms, it represents our *conceived values;*[5] in other terms, our *sacred values,* or "the things really worth fighting for." In order to understand our current value system in operation, it is necessary to examine, however briefly, the main values supported by the creed and the stresses and strains to which those values are liable.

Democracy

As a general value, democracy implies that the experience of the many is more indicative than the experience of the few, that what people want is what they need, and that the people are the best judge of their needs. It implies, further, the right to hold wrong opinions and the right to the familiar freedoms of speech, press, assembly, and organization. But as Tocqueville observed more than a century ago, and as has been observed periodically since, the contrast between the principle of democracy and its practice is nowhere as sharp as in certain aspects of American life.

Individualism

As a general value, individualism implies that the individual is the fountainhead of energy, initiative, and responsibility in society. Politically, it means subservience of the government to the citizenry; organizationally, it means the dominance of humane over bureaucratic attitudes; economically, it means free enterprise based on individual risk; morally, it means that man is a free agent to live his life in his own way. But, again, we must mark the loss between the dream and the deed. We value individualism, but fear personal individuality. We value personal initiative, but are given to chasing the bandwagon. We value individual responsibility, but insist on social conformity. Where in our land, asked that underread and overmaligned Port Huron statement, may one do his own thing with impunity, even when it does no harm to anyone?[6]

Equality

Tocqueville, among other detached observers like Myrdal, marked this as perhaps the most fundamental American value. He wrote, "In America, no one is degraded because he works, for everyone about him works also . . . . In the United States, professions are more or less laborious, more or less profitable, but they are never either high or low; every honest calling is honorable."[7] This is of course an overstatement, yet equality is one of the values of the creed. Tocqueville also noted, however, that democratic institutions awaken and foster a passion for equality they cannot satisfy in practice. A generation ago Myrdal pointed precisely to this as the "American Dilemma," a dilemma that is as characteristic of us today as it was then.

Human Perfectability

As Naegele states: "To be basically hopeful, because the future counts and the past can be forgotten, even rejected, is defiantly cherished by all of us."[8] Yet this optimism must not be confused with joyousness. Our national genius is Mark Twain, both the comic public figure and the bitter private person, and Riesman's title for us, *The Lonely Crowd,* is not without point. As Lynd observed,

> The reverse side of the optimistic dream is woven of trouble. This is a thing we don't talk about. . . . A society as determined as ours to be optimistic imposes false faces on all of us . . . To the greeting "How are you?" the answer must be a confident and hearty "Fine." . . . With us the simple admission of discouragement and a troubled mind is often withheld from our closest friends. In a culture in which to be unsuccessful means automatically to be in some wise a failure, one tends perforce to struggle with one's black moods alone and unaided.[9]

More recently, the Port Huron statement also spoke to this. Despite our presumed limitless potential and riches, "loneliness, estrangement, isolation describe the vast distance between man and man today."[10]

These then, notwithstanding the manifest stresses and strains to which they are liable, are our sacred national values: democracy, equality, individualism, and human perfectability. These are the values that the schools have customarily dealt with and that spring to mind at once when one speaks of American values in a civics or social studies class. They are the values that all of us cherish and want our children to cherish; at least, we feel that we and they *ought* to cherish them. As Myrdal observed, "All means of intellectual communication are utilized to stamp them into everybody's mind. The schools teach them. The churches preach them."[11] They are hammered into easily remembered formulas without any reservation or qualification, and without room for inquiry into what the slogans mean in practice.

Even those in our society who suffer the greatest indignities are not an exception to the general patterns. In the words of Ralph Bunche, "Every man in the street, white, black, red or yellow knows this is 'the land of the free,' the 'land of opportunity,' the 'cradle of liberty,' the 'home of democracy,' that the American flag symbolizes the 'equality of all men' and guarantees to us all 'the protection of life, liberty, and property,' freedom of speech, freedom of religion, and racial tolerance."[12]

TRADITIONAL SECULAR VALUES: THE CLASSIC IMAGE

In a sense, however, we stand in relation to these sacred values as we do to the Ten Commandments or the Golden Rule; at the moment when we may be departing from them most directly, we would be maintaining that we support them most firmly. Was there ever a war that we fought, however ambiguous the purpose, that was not fought in the name of democracy? Just as it is impossible to understand our Christian culture by reading only the precepts of the Bible, so it is impossible to understand the American culture in which the child finds himself, in and out of school, by knowing only the national creed or our sacred values.

For, at another level, there is a core of day-to-day or down-to-earth beliefs that constitute our *operative,* or what I shall call our *secular* values. In effect, if I may overstate the case somewhat, we pay homage to the sacred values on Sundays and state occasions, but in our day-to-day activities we reflect our secular values.

Traditionally, the major secular values—the values that justified, or at least rationalized, our means, modes, and ends of action at work, at play, and in school—were:

The work-success ethic. Values of achievement took precedence over values of being. Anyone could get to the top if he tried hard enough, and everyone had an obligation to try hard enough. Our nobility was the nobility of making it, and success could excuse one for having intermittently broken the Golden Rule or the sacred values. School was a place that was supposed to help one make it; it was the "first rung up the ladder of success." It was no accident that by far the motive most widely studied by researchers in America and its schools was the "Achievement Motive."

Future-time orientation. The future, not the past or even the present, was important. We were constantly to look and move forward. Time, therefore, was held to be a value in its own right, and it became equated with money. (Note: "Time is money.") The present was undervalued for the sake of the future, and immediate gratifications were denied for greater gratifications to come. In school one was supposed gladly to suffer through geometry now in order to enjoy being an engineer later.

Independence or the separate self. One's primary responsibility was to one's self, and the self was of greater ultimate importance than the group. Self-determination, self-activity, self-perfection—the self-made man—these were the criteria of worth. Life was a race, and the reward was to the swift. For every winner there had to be a loser. In school we marked on the curve; for every "A" there had to be an "F."

Puritan morality. Respectability, cleanliness, thrift, self-denial, hard work—these were the marks of common decency. To be sure, there was the holiday, the time for "fun" and "sociability." But this was kept outside the values of everyday living. A vacation was rationalized as the replenishment of energy, a good investment, as it were, for the serious and hence more significant aspects of life. Sociability for the sake of sociability was held to be akin to sloth, and sloth was a sin second only to idolatry. Behind the first-grade teacher's desk were three signs; one learned their import before learning to read. One sign said, "A penny saved is a penny earned"; the second, "If you don't succeed at first, try, try again"; and the third, "Cleanliness is next to Godliness."[13]

TRANSITIONAL SECULAR VALUES: THE 1950s

Despite stresses and strains, the sacred values have remained relatively stable over time. We still go to war in the name of democracy; we still invoke individualism to legitimize industrial conglomerates; nor would many deny equality and human perfectability as ideals for ourselves and our children.

But the traditional operating or secular values underwent transformation, as numerous studies during the 1950s showed, and the transformations had far-reaching consequences for the schools. Riesman, from a *sociological* perspective, first called attention to these transformations at the social level by suggesting that there had been a change from our former inner-directed to prevailing other-directed values.[14] From a *psychoanalytic* perspective, Wheelis, in *The Quest for Identity,* called attention to the same transformations as being a change from our former institutional to the ensuing instrumental values.[15] And Spindler from an *anthropological* perspective identified the transformations as a cultural shift from traditional to emergent values.[16] These several perspectives converged to show a number of crucial changes in the *traditional* American secular value. I should like to call the emerging value pattern, for reasons that will become apparent, a *transitional* one.

From Work-Success to Sociability

The work-success ethic was replaced by an overriding concern for sociability and good public relations as values. The hardworking, self-made Horatio Alger hero gave way to the genial young man in the gray flannel suit as a national model for the young. The important question asked of children in school was not how hard they worked but how happy they were.

Let me cite just one empirical study from this period. This study was reported in *Fortune* magazine in 1956.[17] Mark the source and date, for the same magazine was to do a similar study a dozen years later,[18] with some startling results. Two hundred seniors in twenty colleges and universities were asked to describe their values and personal goals. *Fortune* published the findings under the evocative title "None of This Ulcer Stuff." The seniors explicitly rejected the ambitions, that is, the work-success ethic, of their fathers and aspired to the more genial aspects of life as their goal. As one senior said, "I am not really interested in one of those big executive jobs. None of this ulcer and breakdown stuff for me—just making money doesn't stack up with keeping your health."[19] School was no longer the place where you took the first step up the ladder; what was at the top hardly seemed worth the sweat of the climb, even if one made it.

From Future-Time Orientation to Present-Time Orientation

Instead of future-time orientation, with its consequent self-denial, there was a hedonistic present-time orientation. "A penny saved is a penny earned" gave way to "No down payment necessary." An article in *Harper's Bazaar* in the mid-1950s reported with shock: "The people principally responsible for our twenty-nine billion dollar installment debt on consumer goods are married couples under thirty; two-thirds of these young families are in debt,"[20] an unheard of condition just a generation before. As for the effect in school, it became hard to convince a student to make a down payment, as it were, in geometry in order to become an engineer later.

From Personal Independence to Group Conformity

Instead of competitive independence and the separate self there was compliance and consensus, not originality but adaptability, not proficiency but popularity. In school the important mode of instruction was group dynamics and the significant measure of worth the sociometric test.

These were the apathetic 1950s on campus, the era between Joe McCarthy and Vietnam, when professors were wishing their students would become more active. Little did they know! William Whyte studied this transformation in industry and coined the term "Organization Man" for the new breed. He urged that, if you were being considered for a job, you would be wise to take the following advice:

> 1. When asked word associations or comments about the world, give the most conventional, run-of-the-mill, pedestrian answer possible.
> 2. When in doubt about the most beneficial answer to any question, repeat to yourself:
> I love my mother and my father, but my father a little bit more.
> I like things pretty well as they are.
> I never worry much about anything.
> I don't care for books or music much.[21]

From Puritan Morality to Moral Relativism

Finally, instead of Puritan morality, there were relativistic moral attitudes without strong personal commitment. Absolute right and wrong became questionable. In a sense, morality became a statistical rather than an ethical concept; morality was whatever a group thought was moral. If I may put it metaphorically, we no longer were certain that cleanliness was next to Godliness, or at least not as certain as we had been, and Godliness itself became a rather indeterminate concept.

EMERGENT SECULAR VALUES: THE 1960s

It is not necessary to include here the details of empirical work of the 1950s bearing on the transformations we have been tracing. I have already referred to the studies by Riesman, Wheelis, Whyte, Spindler, and the *Fortune* survey; there were others along the same lines.[22] Nor is it necessary to deal with the contrary argument by Lipset, except to note that there is a contrary argument.[23] But something must be said about the empirical work at the University of Chicago during the mid-1950s, since it bears directly on the subsequent reexamination of the issues.[24]

In 1955 a group of my students and I attempted to study the domain of value just described through interviews and questionnaires in the school setting. We found that interview questions and questionnaire items geared to what I have called traditional and transitional (which at the time, following Spindler, we called "emergent") values covered the subject reasonably well. Samples of students, parents, teachers, principals, and other groups responded to the inquiries willingly and meaningfully. The results were quite consistent with the argument. The values of students were more transitional, while those of their parents were more traditional.[25] The values of younger adults were more transitional, while those of older adults were more traditional.[26] The values of younger teachers and principals were more transitional, while those of older teachers and principals were more traditional,[27] and so on. Moreover, a number of systematic and intriguing relationships were found between the values of pupil, teacher, and principal and the operation of the schools.[28]

We shall return to these value and school relationships in due course. My point here is only to suggest that the values included in the interviews and questionnaires of the time seemed appropriate. They were responded to meaningfully and produced systematic and what we thought were sensible results.

In the late 1960s, some fifteen years after the first series of studies, a number of students and I attempted to examine the values prevailing at the time in the terms given by the preceding traditional-transitional values formulation. I thought it would be a simple matter to apply the same questions used with similar groups earlier and to compare the results.

I was mistaken. The values included in the original design, which were appropriate at that time, were not, or at least not equally, applicable at the later time. A different parameter of values seemed to have been interposed during the intervening years, a parameter not included in the formulations of Riesman, Wheelis, Spindler, Whyte, the *Fortune* survey, and the earlier Chicago studies. For many young people choices that were meaningful based on earlier values were no longer choices at all.

To cite only a single example among many, one of the original items required a respondent to indicate his preference for "The most important thing in school should be to gain knowledge useful to me in the future" (that is, future-time orientation as a value) as against "The most important thing in school should be to learn to get along with other people" (that is, sociability as a value). The item had not been questioned by the respondents fifteen years before. Some chose one alternative, and some chose the other. In interviews each group had seemed happy with the choice they had made and gave what seemed to them sensible reasons for it. Fifteen years later the students objected that neither alternative was sensible or represented their values. As one student said with asperity: "The most important thing in school should not be to gain knowledge useful just to me at some future time, and it should not be how to learn to get along with some other people; it should be how to make a better world for everyone right now."

In short, for numerous young people, especially in college, traditional values (the work-success ethic, future-time orientation, the separate self, Puritan morality) seemed to have become as out of date and unacceptable as the Model T, and the altered values of the late 1940s and early 1950s (sociability, present-time orientation, conformity, and moral relativism) were seen as transitional, indeed as transitory and ephemeral as the fraternity and sorority panty raids and the stuffing of people into telephone booths that occurred during the same period.

What values, then, replaced the earlier ones? In a paper attempting to answer this question presented at a meeting of the International Studies Association in 1970, I wrote that we were yet too close to the phenomenon to speak to it with any certainty.[29] Surely it was too soon to produce the kind of "hard," even if inconclusive, data available on the traditional and transitional values. Nonetheless, a number of observations from different sources converged to permit a reformulation of the secular values pattern, at least as a hypothesis for test by historical hindsight.

When I examined the Port Huron Statement of 1962,[30] the relevance of which was so underestimated at the time, and student documents and editorials in college and secondary school newspapers; when I considered the values expressed in dormitory bull sessions and classroom discussions; when I noted the appearance of student cooperatives, communes, and such movements as Women's Liberation; when I listened to what was being said by a new and, it seemed at the time, growing generation of militants in the ghettos of our cities; when I observed the thousands who came from all over the country to join with Martin Luther King in front of the capitol at Montgomery after the march from Selma; when I compared such studies as the contemporaneous *Fortune* survey (surely this was not a radical sheet) with the similar *Fortune* survey of fifteen years before (compare only the titles: "The College Senior: 'None of this Ulcer Stuff,' " as opposed to "American Youth: Its Outlook Is Changing the World"); and when I added to these the failure of my own attempts to work within the prior terms, I came to the following reformulation in secular values, at least as a hypothesis worthy of investigation.

First, the traditional work-success ethic, which shifted to the ethic of sociability, was modified to an ethic of *social responsibility.* The data from the *Fortune* survey were revealing. Three groups of young people were studied: those not in college, those in college for practical-vocational purposes, and those in college identified as individuals whose views would become more prevalent in the years ahead and whom the survey called "Forerunners." To the question, "Which of these definitions reflect your own personal values?" 75 percent of the Noncollege group, 54 percent of the Practical College group, and only 36 percent of the Forerunner group responded: "Living the good Christian life." The response of 49 percent of the Noncollege group, 53 percent of the Practical College group, and fully 71 percent of the Forerunner group was: "Bringing about needed change in society."[32]

Second, the traditional *future-time* orientation as a value, which shifted to *present-time* orientation as a value, was modified to *relevance* as a value. The Port Huron statement was quite explicit: "[What we want is a] quality [of life] which has full, spontaneous access to present and past experiences, one which easily unites the fragmented parts of personal history, one which openly faces problems which are troubling and unresolved."[33] The *Fortune* survey supports this view. It quotes the composite of Forerunner interviews in this respect as follows: "Our choices are foreclosed from the start. We are taught not what is *relevant,* but what others choose."[34] When asked "What would have a very great influence in your choice of a career?"

57 percent of the Noncollege group, 58 percent of the Practical College group, and only 21 percent of the Forerunner group responded, "Money that can be earned." The response of 55 percent of the Noncollege group, 71 percent of the Practical College group, and fully 80 percent of the Forerunner group was: "Opportunity to make a meaningful contribution."[35]

Third, the traditional value of independence, defined as the separate self, which shifted to conformity as a value, was redefined as meaningful independence and transformed into personal *authenticity* as a value. The Port Huron statement again made the point quite explicitly: "The goal of man and society should be human independence: a concern not with image or popularity but finding a *meaning* in life that is personally *authentic.*"[36] The composite of interviews in *Fortune* stated: "[Our parents] fill their emptiness with material goods and forget human values. They pay lip service to their ideals and overlook the hypocrisy all around them. . . . They have lost control over their lives. . . . We want a society that tolerates candor and spontaneity. We want to retain control over our own lives." Asked the question "Which definitions . . . reflect your own personal values?" 58 percent of the Noncollege group, 57 percent of the Practical College group, and 73 percent of the Forerunner group answered: "Doing your own thing."

Finally, the traditional value of Puritan morality, which shifted to moral relativism as a value, moved toward idealism and became *moral commitment* as a value. The Port Huron statement is again to the point: "The search for truly democratic alternatives to the present, and a commitment to social experimentation with them, is a worthy and fulfilling human enterprise. . . . Theoretic chaos has replaced the idealistic thinking of old—and unable to reconstitute theoretic order, men have condemned idealism itself. . . . To be idealistic [that is, to be morally committed] is considered apocalyptic, deluded. To have no serious aspirations [that is, to be morally relativistic], on the contrary, is to be 'tough-minded.'"[39] To the question in the *Fortune* survey "Are you or your parents more likely to do something about what you believe to be right?" the Noncollege group, the Practical College Group, and the Forerunner group all felt they, more than their parents, would do something about what they believed to be right.[40] In my own conversations with students at the time, this was often expressed as the central emerging value, or at least the most serious quest: moral commitment, a commitment they felt their parents did not possess either because the Puritan values held by some were too trivial and hypocritical or because the relativistic values held by others provided no convictions capable of guiding action.

AMBIGUITY IN VALUES: THE PRESENT

I ended the paper on which the preceding section is based—recall, the paper was written in the late 1960s—with the following sentences:

> It is impossible to say whether the predicated transformations will "take"—whether the emergent values will not be frustrated by those whom the young call the hard hats of the Establishment, or be betrayed by the self-serving excesses of those within their own ranks whom they call the crazies, or be smothered by an apathy engendered through what at least some of the students I talked to feel is the painful futility of their efforts. We are too close to the events to settle these questions, and I suppose we shall resolve them ultimately only through the hindsight of history.[41]

After less than a decade, it is still too soon to talk about the hindsight of history. Yet one cannot avoid the evidence from all sides that there have been changes since the 1960s. Perhaps an anecdote representative of many such will serve to make the point.[42] Susan, a student at the Irvine campus of the University of California, left college in the late 1960s. Like many others, she returned recently for a graduate degree. She was asked, and agreed, to organize a student movement against a law that would disenfranchise students by preventing them from registering to vote at their university home.

Petition in hand, she worked her way through the dormitories. In her words: "It was awful. There wasn't the slightest interest among these students in what was being taken from them. They weren't aware, and they didn't want to listen to me. I came away defeated. I just couldn't believe the changes that have taken place in college students in the last few years."[43]

The anecdote was related by a member of the faculty at Irvine, who also tells of a letter written by a high school civics teacher in a Los Angeles newspaper: "The majority of young people with whom I come in contact was never enthralled by politics. Now, they seem to be sinking even deeper into an apolitical torpor. Watergate taught them not to care. I see the silent majority growing in my classroom every school day. It is a frightening development."[44]

Other evidence, the professor at Irvine points out, is all around. When the University of California at San Diego opened a new school recently that stressed "professional and preprofessional training," it was immediately oversubscribed while admissions were generally declining elsewhere. As the provost explained, the response was due to "a new breed of student who is thinking more about jobs, money, and the future."

An experience by the professor at a talk he gave to social science classes in a local high school is also revealing. His daughter had been a student at the same school when President Kennedy was assassinated. When she heard about it, she walked out of the school and several miles to the ocean, where she sat alone until darkness drove her home. Speaking to students at the same school a decade later, he assumed similar awarenesses and interests that had been present in his daughter's day. He soon realized that he and the students were not even "on the same planet." So he tried to penetrate, as he says, "the glaze over their eyes" with more and more outrageous statements, hoping for some kind of response. *Anything* at all. But to no avail.

The denouement may be stated best in his own words: "When nothing came back, I began asking them questions. And, slowly, I began to see that I was dealing with students who had happily accepted the social and political changes won by the activists of the 1960s and totally discarded the commitments that produced the changes. At last I asked these students if they would demonstrate if we started massive bombing of Vietnam again tomorrow. Nothing. In desperation, I said: 'For God's sake, what *would* outrage you?' After a pause, a girl in the front row wearing a cheerleader uniform raised her hand and said tentatively, 'Well, I'd be pretty mad if they bombed this *school.*' "

The writer recognized, as should we, that this is one upper-middle-class high school in a conservative area of California and that generalizing from a single experience is dangerous. Yet, as he also points out, from this same background came young people who marched in Mississippi and unseated a President of the United States in New Hampshire, who demanded and got long overdue educational reforms, who broke down outmoded social castes and attitudes. He went on to say:

> True, they also disrupted classes, undermined useful social values and traditions, loved the sounds of their own voices, and frequently substituted rhetoric for reason and self-indulgent impulse for effective action. They were noisy and abrasive, and when it was all over I was relieved. For a while.
>
> But now I contemplate the reaction—I wonder about our future. Now I'm told to honk if I love Jesus. I hear students dismiss Watergate as "the way it's always been, so why hassle it?" I see them single-mindedly pursuing grades and worrying about jobs with secure retirement plans. I even see a resurgence of those pillars of the American social caste system, fraternities and sororities.[45]

I dare say this is not true, or at least not as true, in all regions of the country, or for all high schools or for all colleges and universities. And surely not for all social classes. Yet a change from the 1960s in palpable, although just what commitments and values this change represents are obscure.[46]

To go back, then, to the issue raised initially, did the emergent values of the 1960s not "take" at all, and have we returned to the traditional and transitional values? An unequivocal answer is not possible. It seems that, in some respects, the emergent values did take, and quite wholly; in others, they took only partially and seem to be drifting back to the traditional state; in still others, they did not take at all, and, after a shift during the 1960s, are now back where they were in the early 1950s and before.

I cite an instance from a college survey illustrating each pattern. The item is: "The federal government should require all employers to hire people without regard to their race, religion, color, or nationality." This item may be taken as roughly representing the emergent value of social responsibility. At a midwestern public university in 1952, only 47 percent agreed; in 1968 fully 80 percent agreed; by 1974 the direction of change was continuing, and 89 percent agreed. The results are the same in an eastern private college where, in 1952, 52 percent agreed; in 1968, 76 percent; and, by 1974, 83 percent.

Consider now this item: "Do you ever get as worked up about something in politics and public affairs as you do about something that happened in your personal life?" The item may be taken as roughly representing the emergent value of moral commitment. In 1952 only 30 percent said "Yes"; in 1968, the height of student activism, fully 68 percent said "Yes"; and, by 1974, the direction was being reversed in that only 61 percent said "Yes."

Finally, consider the item: "Government planning almost inevitably results in the loss of essential liberties and freedoms." At the eastern private college, in 1952 there were 30 percent who agreed; in 1969, only 15 percent; by 1974, 27 percent—almost back to the attitude of the 1950s. This pattern is repeated at the midwestern public university, giving added support to the data. In 1952, 30 percent agreed; in 1969, there was a drop to 24 percent; by 1974, an increase to 32 percent—ever surpassing the earlier figure.

The data raise some interesting questions. Why, for example, did some of the emergent values take wholly, others somewhat, and still others, after an initial change, revert to the former state? But this is not pertinent here. Rather, the point is, first, that both the anecdotal and survey data support the idea of value change. Second, and even more important in the present context, the data suggest the source of uncertainty in current values. To use the items regarding social responsibility as representative of other values as well, in the 1960s the answers to all items pointed consistently in the direction of greater social responsibility and conviction. By 1974 this was no longer true. It would appear that the responses to the several items go off in several directions—sometimes toward greater and sometimes toward lesser responsibility and conviction.[48] There is confusion or at least uncertainty in commitment, and the crucial question at this time for the young (as for their elders) may well be: *What,* if any, are the values?

By way of summary, Table 4-1 outlines the apparent alternations over time in the status of what we have called our secular values. (The dates, of course, represent only the most tentative of benchmarks.)

Table 4-1
Transformation in National Secular Values

Traditional values (classical American image)	Transitional values (late 1940s to mid-1950s)	Emergent values (middle to late 1960s)	What values? (mid-1970s)[a]
Work-success ethic	Sociability	Social responsibility	?
Future-time orientation	Present-time orientation	Relevance	?
Independence	Conformity	Authenticity	?
Puritan morality	Moral relativism	Moral commitment	?

[a]Readers may wish to substitute appropriate values for the question marks, or, for that matter, elsewhere in the table.

The classification of values in four categories is arbitrary; one may add other values or subtract some, for the compulsively tidy scheme is intended to be illustrative, not definitive. The catchwords for the values are only shorthand designations and are to be understood with due regard for the inevitable hazards of naming. And of course in this macroscopic view of values, I have scarcely been able to do more than hint at the complexities of more microscopic and much-needed views of values by region, class, sex, education, and so forth.

The periods demarcated by the benchmark dates were by no means so sharply defined as the necessarily schematic account unavoidably implies; at any given time it was a question of relative emphasis rather than the all-or-none presence or absence of a particular value. Surely Puritan morality did not disappear on a given day, and moral relativism appear. Nonetheless, a little content analysis of basal readers, wherein I compared a *McGuffey Reader* of the 1910s with *My Little Red Story Book* of the 1940s, and with *Get Set* of the 1970s, reveals a quite remarkable isomorphism with traditional, transitional, and emergent values. The *McGuffey Reader* stresses work and virtue, *My Little Red Story Book* stresses sociability and play, and *Get Set* includes blacks and slums (recall Sally, Dick, Jane, and Spot).

VALUES IN THE SCHOOL SETTING

Values pervade every aspect of the school. I cite by way of illustration only a sampling from systematic observations. (*a*) As already noted, curriculum materials vary in the values they reflect—witness the values explicitly or implicitly represented even in basal readers.[49] (*b*) Schools vary in the dominant values held by their teachers, so that pupils in one school are exposed to a different set of values than if they were in another school.[50] (*c*) Schools vary in the dominant values held by their pupils, so that teachers in one school are faced with a different set of values than if they were in another school. (*d*) Along with the between-school group differences are within-school individual differences among pupils, teachers, and principals. (*e*) When pupils and teachers hold similar values, whether of one kind or another, the pupils tend to rate their teachers more favorably; when they hold dissimilar values, the pupils tend to rate their teachers less favorably. This is true despite the fact that pupils are exposed to the same manifest behavior of the same teachers in the same classrooms. (*f*) The reverse has also been observed. When the values of pupils and of teachers are similar, the teachers tend to rate the pupils more favorably by letter grade than when the values are dissimilar, despite the fact that the pupils did equally well on an objective achievement test (of which the teachers were unaware). (*g*) The achievement of pupils is significantly related to the values they hold, even when intelligence and social class are controlled. (*h*) The occupational choices and career aspirations of secondary school students are significantly related to their values.

It is clear that values pervade the school. But the crucial question remains: If the matter of values is so critical both to what children do in school and their aspirations in life, is the school having any systematic effect on the nature of the values they acquire?

The research designated to answer this question was straightforward. The traditional-transition values instrument to which I have already referred was administered to freshmen and seniors in sixteen public high schools, four religious high schools, and two private high schools. The results were unequivocal. Differences in values were found among the different high schools, showing that the instrument did in fact discriminate among groups. But within each type of school, whatever the type of school, *there were no significant differences between the values held by freshmen and the values held by seniors.*[51]

The results seemed quite remarkable. They may have been the result of the cross-sectional nature of the study, that is, the freshmen and seniors were different individuals who were tested at the same time. So another investigator undertook a longitudinal study in ten high schools. That is, the freshmen and seniors were the same individuals tested during their first and last years in school. The results were essentially the same: differences among different types of schools, but no differences at all between freshmen and seniors in nine of the ten schools for males, and little change for females in four of the ten schools.[52]

It would appear that, whatever values children brought with them when they entered a particular school, they also took away with them when they left. This conclusion holds at least for the types of values represented in the instrument used, even though other types of values (for example, appreciation of the arts) may have changed. And neither the private nor the religious nor the public school seemed to be more effective or less effective than any other in this respect.

CONTINUITIES AND DISCONTINUITIES IN VALUES BETWEEN SCHOOL AND CHILD

Although no definitive reason can be given for the failure of schools to influence markedly the values of children, the following suggestion is worth considering as one possibility. All children acquire their fundamental "codes for future learning" or "learning sets" in the family during the period ascribed to primary socialization.[53] One of the sets is the *language code;* the other is the *value code.* The language code gives the child categories for structuring and communicating experiences. The value code tells the child which experiences are important. In a sense, language becomes the medium through which children perceive and express experience, and values determine what in their experience they will accept or reject.

Typically, school requires an achievement ethic that sets a high value on the future, deferred gratification, and symbolic commitment to success. It assumes that every child has had an opportunity to acquire beliefs that anyone can get to the top if he tries hard enough and that, if he tries, he, too, can reach the top. The future, not the present, is what counts, and one must use the present to prepare for the future. Time is valuable and must not be wasted ("Time is money."), and the school assumes that timed tests carry the same urgency for everyone. It is expected that the pupil will be able to defer gratification through symbolic commitment to success; he will study geometry now to become an engineer later, as was said earlier.

These are not only the values of the school; they are also the values of the families in which many of the children are reared. These children acquire from the earliest years a value code compatible with school values just as they acquire a language code compatible with school language. There is no reason for them to change, and the school provides no model for change.

In contrast to this, other children have experienced what is primarily a survival or subsistence ethic, which sets a high value on the present rather than the future, on immediate rather than deferred gratification, on concrete rather than symbolic commitment. Where these children live, hardly anyone ever gets to the top; one often cannot even move across the street. Time is not important or potentially valuable if there is not going to be anything to do with it anyway. And what does an appeal to symbolic success mean where the only success the child has seen can be measured only in terms of subsistence and survival? These children face severe discontinuities in values when they come to school—discontinuities that may have a profound effect on their behavior toward school and the school's behavior toward them.

Such children are often accused of failing in school because they are intellectually apathetic and physically aggressive. It might be more accurate to question whether they may not be intellectually apathetic and physically aggressive because they fail. For what can be more tormenting than to be confronted day after day with a situation in which language and value codes seem different in inexplicable ways from those to which you are accustomed, and, more, a situation in which you cannot succeed and from which you are not permitted to escape without threat of severe punishment?

Reaction to this type of frustration is hopelessness and rage. In school, the hopelessness is manifested in apathy and intellectual withdrawal from the source of frustration; the rage is expressed as aggression and physical attack upon the source of frustration. These are not conditions in which learning can take place, especially not the learning of new values.

VALUES AND THE PREPARATION AND PLACEMENT OF TEACHERS

In view of these circumstances, customary teacher preparation and placement procedures are dysfunctional. There is little difference between the preparation of teachers for one locality and the preparation of teachers for another. Distinctions in training and placement are all vertical, that is, for one specific age-grade or another; they are not horizontal, that is, for the same grade but in different localities.

Yet even a cursory visit to Woodlawn and Winnetka (or Harlem and Scarsdale) reveals that the differences in teaching the same grade—say, eighth—in Woodlawn and Winnetka are infinitely greater than teaching two different grades—say, eighth and ninth—in the one locality or the other. Despite this, the teachers for the eighth and ninth grades were prepared in different types of teacher-training programs, but the teachers for localities as different as Woodlawn and Winnetka were prepared in the same types of teacher-training programs. This failure to differentiate between teacher-training programs by locality of the school in addition to the age of the pupils is why so many teachers do not perform effectively in so many of our schools. They not only cannot cope with the children's values, but they cannot cope with their own commitments when confronted with the children's values.

We all know of cases in which generous, sensitive, and humane teachers have established schools in neighborhoods where, until then, the atmosphere had been one of terror, threats, and outright violence directed against the instructors. Within a year, these desperate youth have, under the influence of loving and understanding teachers, replaced suspicion with trust, hostility with affection, and cynicism and selfishness with openness and helping.[54]

But even these achievements, remarkable as they are, seem to be accompanied by nagging, troublesome questions about values. The teachers in these schools ask themselves whether they have simply imposed their values, possibly at the risk of rendering their students unfit in their fight for survival. In the metaphor of one report of such a school: "Have we disabled these survivors of the jungle by domestication?"[55]

The teachers wonder, too, whether they have merely substituted their goals for those of the students and, to achieve those goals, constructed a curriculum that may be a subtle act of aggression against their students, a curriculum that does not seriously, sympathetically, and objectively weigh what is of merit in the culture of those students. As the same report asks: "A curriculum for what, and for whom?"[56] The present circumstance in the schools seems to be that insensitive and thoughtless educators do not bother to ask: "What values?" Even the sensitive and thoughtful ones who do ask are uncertain, or at least apologetic, about the answer.

THE SCHOOL AS SOCIALIZER: WHAT VALUES?

The human organism is not born into the world with a ready-made set of culturally adaptive behaviors and values.[57] Instead, he must acquire them. He must inevitably learn to put the question to himself: "May I yield to the impulse within me, or will I, by doing so, imperil the highest values of my society?" He must learn, on the one hand, to suppress or to modify certain of his drives. He must learn, on the other hand, to acquire certain culturally adaptive attitudes and values. One of the functions of the school has customarily been to help the child do just this.

But the word "learning" or "schooling" is something of a euphemism here, for it is not the same kind of learning as, say, memorizing the multiplication tables, or the capitals of the states, or the pledge of allegiance. The child's learning, or, perhaps better here, the interiorizing of social values, is a much more intimate and complex process. Learning, imitation, conscious emulation play a part, to be sure. But a fundamental mechanism by which we interiorize values in school as elsewhere is *identification.*[58] As the child struggles to integrate and to maintain a stable self-image from among his fragmentary perceptions of who he is and where he belongs, he is led to view himself as at one with another person. The parents are the child's earliest objects of identification. Later he may add older siblings, favorite neighbors, community heroes, certain members of his peer group, and, of course, school personnel. In making these identifications, the child not only assumes the outward manners and expressive movements of his "significant figures," but attempts also to incorporate their values and attitudes as well.

It is in this context that the school situation can acquire an eminence second only to the home perhaps—an eminence that it certainly does not have now. To be sure, many aspects of the child's personality and values are already formed by the time he enters school. But the way in which these aspects are developed and modified may depend on the character of the educational institution of which he becomes a part. The teachers become, or at least can become, significant figures for the child. But where values are concerned, it is not so much what people *say* the child should do as the kinds of models the significant figures provide that are important.

When we find ourselves in a period of rapidly changing values, the various significant others in the school and community provide uncertain and inconsistent, if not contradictory, models for the child. The problem, of course, is not the variety of values, which is not only inevitable but desirable. The problem, rather, is that the values are latent and unexamined; the ambiguities and differences are often invisible and underground, as it were.

In such a situation, if identification occurs at all, it provokes conflict and anxiety. For to identify with one model means knowingly, or even worse unknowingly, to reject another model. To accept the parent's values may mean to reject the teacher's values; to accept the teacher's values may mean to reject the religious leader's values; to accept the religious leader's values may mean to reject the political leader's values; to accept the political leader's values may mean to reject the very values parents, teachers, and religious leaders are advocating.

As a result the child, consciously or subconsciously, finds it extraordinarily difficult to adapt. The solution may be to seek safety in the inflexible incorporation of one model or in the renunciation of all models. In the one case we have *overidentification,* with consequent restrictions and rigidity of purpose; in the other we have *underidentification,* with consequent confusion and purposelessness. Both represent serious inadequacy in personal development as a result of inadequacies in prevailing models and values. While we are loudly urging our children to acquire appropriate values in school, the children may more properly—albeit mutely—be asking the school: "*What* values?"

NOTES

1. Portions of this paper are based on Jacob W. Getzels, "Changing Values Challenge the Schools," *School Review* 65 (March 1957): 92-102; *id.*, "The Acquisition of Values in School and Society," in *The High School in a New Era*, ed. Francis S. Chase and Harold A. Anderson (Chicago: University of Chicago Press, 1958), 146-161; *id.*, "On the Transformation of Values: A Decade after Port Huron," *School Review* 80 (August 1972): 505-519; *id.*, "Socialization and Education: A Note on Discontinuities," *Teachers College Record* 76 (December 1974): 218-225.

2. Clyde Kluckhohn *et al.*, "Values and Value-Orientation in the Theory of Action," in *Toward a General Theory of Action*, ed. Talcott Parsons and Edward Shils (Cambridge, Mass.: Harvard University Press, 1952), 395.

3. I am indebted for many of the formulations and sources in this section of the chapter to an unpublished memorandum by Professor Kaspar Naegele, who very kindly permitted me to make use of the material.

4. Gunnar Myrdal, *An American Dilemma: The Negro Problem and Modern Democracy* (New York: Harper Torchbooks, 1962), I, 3.

5. Charles William Morris, *Varieties of Human Value* (Chicago: University of Chicago Press, 1956).

6. See "From the Port Huron Statement," in *The New Student Left: An Anthology*, ed. Mitchell Cohen and Dennis Hale (Boston, Mass.: Beacon Press, 1966), 10-13.

7. Alexis de Tocqueville, *Democracy in America* (Cambridge, Mass.: Sever and Francis, 1864), II, 185-186.

8. See note 3, above.

9. Robert S. Lynd, in the preface to Earl L. Koos, *Families in Trouble* (New York: King's Crown Press, 1946), vii-viii.

10. "From the Port Huron Statement," 13.

11. Myrdal, *American Dilemma*, 4.

12. *Ibid.*

13. The classification and analysis of "traditional" and "emergent" values of the 1950s are based in part on George D. Spindler, "Education in a Transforming American Culture," *Harvard Educational Review* 25 (No. 3, 1955): 145-153.

14. David Riesman *et al.*, *The Lonely Crowd* (New Haven, Conn.: Yale University Press, 1950).

15. Allen Wheelis, *The Quest for Identity* (New York: W. W. Norton and Co., 1958).

16. Spindler, "Education in a Transforming American Culture."

17. "The College Senior: 'None of this Ulcer Stuff,' " *Fortune* 45 (October 1956): 155.

18. "American Youth: Its Outlook Is Changing the World," special issue of *Fortune* 79 (January 1969).

19. "The College Senior."

20. Caroline Bird, "Born 1930: The Unlost Generation," *Harper's Bazaar* 90 (February 1957): 106.

21. William H. Whyte, Jr., "Beware of Your Personality," *Encounter* 7 (August 1956): 17.

22. See Henry S. Commager, *The American Mind* (New Haven, Conn.: Yale University Press, 1950); Max Lerner, *America as a Civilization: Life and Thought in the United States Today* (New York: Simon and Schuster, 1956).

23. Seymour M. Lipset and Leo Lowenthal, *Culture and Social Character: The*

Work of David Riesman Reviewed (Glencoe, Ill.: Free Press, 1961); see especially "A Changing American Character?" 136-171.

24. For references and brief descriptions of some of the studies, see Jacob W. Getzels, James M. Lipham, and Roald F. Campbell, *Educational Administration as a Social Process* (New York: Harper and Row, 1968), 286-297.

25. Shelley C. Stone, "A Study of the Relationship among Values, Family Characteristics, and Personality Variables of Adolescents," unpub. diss., University of Chicago, 1960.

26. Roderick F. McPhee, "The Relationship between Individual Values, Educational Viewpoint, and Local School Approval," unpub. diss., University of Chicago, 1959.

27. Richard Prince, "A Study of the Relationship between Individual Values and Administrative Effectiveness in the School Situation," unpub. diss., University of Chicago, 1957.

28. Getzels, Lipham, and Campbell, *Educational Administration as a Social Process,* 286-297.

29. Getzels, "On the Transformation of Values."

30. "From the Port Huron Statement," 10-13.

31. See the articles from *Fortune* magazine, cited in notes 17 and 18, above.

32. "What They Believe," *Fortune* 79 (January 1969): 179.

33. "From the Port Huron Statement," 12-13.

34. Gregory H. Wierzynski, "A Student Declaration: Our Most Wrenching Problem. . . ," *Fortune* 79 (January 1969): 115.

35. "What They Believe," 181.

36. "From the Port Huron Statement," 12 [italics mine].

37. Wierzynski, "A Student Declaration," 114.

38. "What They Believe," 179.

39. "From the Port Huron Statement," 10-11.

40. "What They Believe," 179.

41. Getzels, "On the Transformation of Values," 517.

42. Joseph N. Bell, "Silence on Campus," *Harper's* 252 (March 1976): 18-24.

43. *Ibid.,* 18.

44. *Ibid.,* 20, for this and the following quotations.

45. *Ibid.*

46. An article appearing in the *New York Times Magazine* for June 26, 1977 (pages 20 ff.), entitled "All's Quiet at Scarsdale High," rather nicely parallels the *Harper's* piece I have been citing. It says in part, "[The students] seem to be organizing their energies, interests, and time around what other people expect of them. . . . They reflect a passivity, uniformity, and materialism reminiscent of the 1950s, the teachers report and observers of the educational scene say they are part of a broad national trend. For example, a recent poll conducted nationally by the National Association of Secondary School Principals concluded that quiet had settled over high school campuses, with students declaring that they are satisfied with their country, families, and schools! It was only a few years ago . . . that Scarsdale students were boycotting grapes to support striking West Coast farm workers, wearing black armbands at graduation to protest the Vietnam War, handing out leaflets for a probusing school board candidate and going on hunger strikes for Biafra. They shared in the social upheavals of the 1960s and raised sharp questions about the values of their parents and their affluent community."

47. Dean R. Hoge, "Changes in College Students' Value Patterns in the 1950s, 1960s, and 1970s" (Washington, D.C.: Boys' Town Center, Catholic University, 1975, mimeo).

48. The turmoil of the 1960s has left residuals in students' behavior in the form of increased use of drugs, alcohol, and greater freedom in sexual activity. It has also left its mark on academic routines: students evaluate their teachers and courses, students' rights to "due process" have been institutionalized, the awareness of opportunities for women has been increased. But the point made by the article in *Harper's* (see note 42, above) and that in the *New York Times Magazine* (see note 46, above) is, as the former states, that the students have "happily accepted the social and political changes won by the activists in the 1960s and totally discarded the commitment that produced the changes" (p. 20).

49. *What Children Read in School: Critical Analysis of Primary Reading Textbooks,* ed. Sara Goodman Zimet (New York: Grune and Stratton, 1972).

50. See the works cited in notes 24, 25, 26, and 27, above, for this and the following observations.

51. See Prince, "Study of the Relationship between Individual Values and Administrative Effectiveness," and Getzels, Lipham, and Campbell, *Educational Administration as a Social Process.*

52. Orville E. Thompson and Sara G. Carr, "Values of High School Students and Their Teachers," Office of Education, Grant no. OE 3-10-052 Report, University of California, Davis, 1966.

53. See Getzels, "Socialization and Education."

54. John Shlien and Ronald F. Levant, "The Robert W. White School," *Harvard Graduate School of Education Association Bulletin* 19 (1974): 12-18.

55. *Ibid.,* 13.

56. *Ibid.,* 17.

57. See Getzels, "Acquisition of Values in School and Society."

58. Erik Erikson, *Childhood and Society* (New York: W. W. Norton and Co., 1950); Max L. Hutt and Daniel R. Miller, "Value Interiorization and Democratic Education," *Journal of Social Issues* 5 (No. 4, 1949): 31-43; Daniel R. Miller and Max L. Hutt, "Value Interiorization and Personality Development," *ibid.,* 2-30.

5. What Happens to Parents

Elizabeth Douvan

Adolescence represents a critical point in socialization for both the child and the family. Our descriptions of the developmental stage have concentrated on the child and, since Erik Erikson's seminal work in the 1950s, have become both more cogent and more articulate about the tasks confronting the child and the mechanisms and processes by which young people make the transition into fully participating membership in the social system.

What we have not looked at with nearly as great concentration and imagination is the other side of the socialization process, the effect of the adolescent child on the parents' socialization. Since the parents' response to their child's adolescence will set the conditions of that experience in many respects, it seems crucial for us to analyze it with the same care that we have applied to the child's side of the process. This is the task I want to address here.

My underlying assumption is that adolescents reflect their broader culture rather than create it. What adolescents are reflects in striking ways what their parents are and what their culture directs them to be. To those social critics like Oscar and Mary Handlin and Midge Decter who decry the directions the youth culture takes, I can only respond by saying: Look to your own values and behavior. We, the adult generation, set the direction and stand for the unspoken assumptions and

---

Reprinted, with permission, from *The Center Magazine* 9 (May-June): 11-15.

values which the young pick up and act out. Each generation creates a new *Zeitgeist* and develops a new tone and style, but each generation of adolescents does so by recombining elements that are provided by the generation of adults.

First, then, . . . look at the interrelation between adolescents and adults, that is, the structure of the relationship within which they socialize each other. The adolescent tasks are by their very nature well designed to exert regressive pulls on parents. Consider two examples:

1. The child at puberty is confronted with a radical restructuring of the internal environment. Gonadal development and the infusion of gonadal hormones into the system stimulate new drives, moods, and fantasies. The psychological problem for the youngster is the integration of these new realities into a developing concept of the self. The fact of adult genital capability requires a restructuring of his interpersonal world and of his experience and expression of love. The adolescent must learn to integrate sex with love and affection. Until this point the incest taboo has required the child to segregate sexual feelings from ties of love, since the significant loves to this point have been members of the child's own family.

The problem for the parents, on the other hand, is to keep sex and love neatly segregated in the face of the child's palpable new sexuality. And this is no easy trick. Here is the parent, accustomed over the years to a relationship of closeness, affection, tenderness with his child—a relationship uncomplicated by sexual conflicts. Now all of a sudden what had been taken for granted and filled with pleasure is disrupted by the subtle intrusion of sexuality. The tickling [and] the sitting on daddy's lap become overcast with a hint of danger, conflict, the need for controls where none previously needed to be invoked.

2. The adolescent task presses the youngster to withdraw cathexis from the family and to reinvest it in the peer group where he experiments in forming and dissolving relationships and group attachments and begins the work of identity formation—of detecting continuity in the self in the face of discontinuity of the interpersonal setting. A side feature of this process—and absolutely necessary as an accumulation of cathexis and energy for the large work of discovering or creating a self—is a significant measure of narcissism. The youngster becomes self-absorbed.

The parents, meanwhile, are exactly at that stage of development in which the self is defined by its roles and relationships to others. They measure themselves by their interdependencies and mutualities. They are nothing if not workers, parents, marriage partners, citizens, friends. The network of interdependent relationships forms, for the generative adult, the meaning of life and the definition of self. When the child pulls out of the family—at least emotionally and perhaps also geographically—the parents are left with their parenting needs and behaviors dangling. They need to parent and they need the parent role as one of their self-defining elements. But there is no longer a child to receive the parenting, no longer a reciprocal to their parent role.

What do parents do in this situation? Ideally they recognize interdependence as a relationship of many forms and say to the child by their behavior: now your needs require a *new* kind of relationship, a new stage of our developing interdependence. You need to have freedom to explore and form yourself outside the bounds of the family. I will give you this freedom, this distance. I will also grant you new recognition as an autonomous being. What you need from me has changed. That you need something remains.

And ideally the child will have the sensitivity and empathy to give the parents room and credit for their new form of parenting.

But things are not always so ideal, and even in the best of circumstances the shift in relationship is likely to be experienced by the parents as a loss. No matter how we phrase it and no matter how likely particular parents are to enjoy a newly based and more adult relationship with their children, the fact is that they have lost the little child and the baby they once enjoyed—their youth, along with the expectations and unjaded hopes they had when that baby was little. The emerging adulthood of one's children must at some level register as the signal of one's own decline.

So parents respond variously when their children withdraw their emotional chips. Some make use of old mechanisms learned in previous encounters in which a threat was posed by the other. They may identify with the child in a paradoxically reversed repetition of their identification in childhood with an overwhelmingly powerful parent. Though the roles are reversed, the threat and the process invoked are the same. They may—as increasing numbers of women have done in the last ten years—return to their own identity task and regroup emotional resources for a new self-investment and self-definition. They may decide to take up painting, or find a new career opportunity, or look to the issue of refurbishing their marriage relationship which, having given and stretched to accommodate children, may by this time have become quite threadbare except in the area of their intense parallel concern with child rearing.

However they respond in the long run, the parents must experience separation from the child—and mourn the loss. Depending on the particular conditions of separation and the extent to which the child's emerging adulthood represents a shocking discrepancy between the parents' aspiration and accomplishment, it will leave the parents either ready to move on to a new stage in the parent role or dashed and disillusioned with life.

In my experience—and despite all of our popular mythology about the controlling mother who cannot give up her children and tries with all her means to keep them dependent—it is fathers who suffer adolescents' separation most acutely. Often, I think, the child's assertion of autonomy comes as a ruder shock to the father who has not been so intimately involved as the mother has in the child's many smaller departures during childhood. It also often comes—this first and final move toward independence—at a time when the father is having to face the fact that he is not going to realize all of his ambitions in work—that point when many men look at themselves in the mirror and ask, "Is this all there is?" The combination of disappointment in work and loss of control of the child can precipitate a crisis or a period of acting out which in turn can lead to dissolution of the family.

I will come back to the family and discuss ways in which both child and parent can be helped to accept the changing nature of their relationship without rejecting the relationship and their interdependence as such. But here, on the level of culture, let us consider ways in which contemporary critics in our society have conceived adolescence and responded to it, and how their views differ from those of other times and other cultures.

What I want to note first in the views of the Handlins, Midge Decter, and other critics of youth is the fact that they no longer assume the narcissism of adolescence to be part of a developmental phase which has clear limits. Their apparent fear is based on the assumption that the features they find appalling in the young—narcissism, marginalism, unwillingness to postpone gratification—are historical phenomena which mark this generation and will continue as their style throughout adulthood and old age. They attach such characteristics to various causal forces—Dr. Benjamin Spock and child-centered techniques of child-rearing, affluence, the liberalism of parents in post-World War II America. But whatever the cause, it is viewed as a historical stamp which distinguishes this generation of young from all which have gone before.

They do not, in other words, attach the traits they dislike to a stage in normal life development but rather to the generation as such and for all of life.

In earlier periods this is not the way people thought about adolescence. People were highly aware of adolescence as a stage, even if they had no name for it. Those who were young yet physically mature, sexual but not included in the institutional structures that allowed legitimate sexual expression, were seen as special, as possessing energy and powers which were without channels in the organized life of the adult community. All recorded societies seem to provide some mechanisms for organizing these powers in the service of the group life or at least of neutralizing their potential for destructiveness. Natalie Davis and other historians have catalogued the courts of misrule and other youth groups and have described their functions.

In the past people complained of youth. We are all familiar with the wonderfully contemporary-sounding quotations from Plato and other philosophers down through the ages inveighing against the young. They all share the general message that the generation about to take over is dissolute, without character, and going to hell in a handcart.

What they do not share with some of today's critics is the latter's finality, a time perspective which extends across the life span. All of the early complaints clearly see adolescence or youth as finite and their problems as eventually dissolving in the responsibilities and privileges of adulthood to which youth will eventually succeed. The traditional complaint was one of timing—that youth were not moving briskly enough to the inevitable next stage in their development. Plato, George Bernard Shaw, and Booth Tarkington all saw the youth of their day as self-centered, self-indulgent, and irresponsible. But they say nothing final or historically absolute about such traits. In their conceptual scheme, youth was a stage with a beginning and an end, and the end of the offending traits would come when this youth cohort, like all cohorts before, took its place as adults. No one doubted that youth would end and adulthood would take over.

What distinguishes contemporary complaints about youth and adds to the weight of anxiety they carry is the sense they have that adulthood may *not* be inevitable, that adolescents may never grow up, that the character of the contemporary cohort of youth may have been marked by historical factors so indelible that youth will never mature but will carry self-absorption and irresponsibility along with them into adulthood and beyond.

Why? Why are we so apprehensive about our young? Why do we doubt that they will grow up just like all previous generations? Is it really, as Midge Decter claims, because our desire to make life beautiful and nurturing for them in childhood was really a cover for lack of commitment—that we made their lives beautiful in order not to have to cross them, to take the role of ultimate authority, and that in essence we abandoned them by this choice?

Or is our fear not perhaps grounded on the fact that our concepts of the goal of growth—adulthood—have become shaky and unclear? In earlier generations people worried less about youth getting stuck at their stage because they could see quite clearly what other generations had come to, they knew that adulthood would overtake the young, and they were satisfied with their vision of what that adulthood would be.

In our time, on the other hand, the image and definition of adulthood has become confused. Does adulthood mean commitment, restraint, mutuality, responsibility, and abandoning the idea of "instant gratification"? But where do we find these characteristics in adult life, and where do we find adults who not only practice such virtues but derive both satisfaction and self-definition from the practice? In the husbands and fathers who leave their families in middle life because they have found their true love and have answered their question, "Is this all there is?" with a resounding "No" and gone off to start a new family? In the women who leave families because they now discover an inner voice or talent which they must realize? In an economic system that urges people to "go now, pay later" and stimulates needs and desires which can only be gratified on an installment plan if at all? In political leaders who excoriate the young for their laziness, lack of ambition, immorality, and searching for the easy way, but all along are themselves accepting bribes and using their high offices to reap illegitimate, easy, and instant rewards? In the adults who frequent encounter groups, vacation at Esalen, and dress like adolescents?

. . . The meaning of adulthood, its gratifications, and its styles have all become muddy. There are, of course, admirable adults who have a sense of their own meaning and are committed and satisfied. But they represent only one model of adulthood, and there are others available, perhaps even dominant, who represent, above all, an anachronistic enshrinement of all the adolescent traits we decry in the young.

This lack of a clear concept of the goal of growth—of any consensual image of adulthood which is both attractive and satisfying—is, I think, what leads our social critics to fear that adolescents may not come out of it, or that they will not know where to go when they reach the end of the adolescent era.

. . . The regularity of this hypocrisy in extreme statements of moral indignation hints at a general rule—that those who accuse most intensely may be driven by some peculiar inner dynamic, that projection may be operating, that attacking others may serve as a defense against one's own tenuously controlled impulses.

And I have found this to be true among those most ready to write off the younger generation as self-indulgent and greedy.

Within the last month I have witnessed two examples. One involved a colleague who recently entered the academic world from business, and was enraged at the idea that he should be evaluated before promotion to a high academic rank. The other was the wife of a colleague who decided after many years in the field to complete a long-abandoned Ph.D. and was offended when she was told that she would have to negotiate the normal admission procedures. Both of these individuals had succeeded in their previous careers and had been rewarded for their success. Yet these legitimate rewards were somehow not all they expected—they thought the previous success should also carry entitlement to instant Ph.D.'s and instant professorships. They did not want to be evaluated when they moved into new spheres. Yet they would be among the first to see irresponsibility in the young, to complain that the young want instant rewards.

Data on the values, attitudes, and personal integrations of youth have been accumulating now for twenty-five to thirty years. The generalization that emerges most clearly from the studies is that, by and large, the values and identities of youth will strongly reflect parental values and identity. In studies of political and religious attitudes, of delinquency, alienation, radicalism, and of broad patterns of adjustment, the results point to the same conclusion. If our children reject the idea of having children, it is because in our parenting of them we have not communicated the joys of parenting. If they do not accept authority unquestioningly, it is because we have taught them to think for themselves. If they are self-indulgent and seek instant gratification, they have access to adult models who are equally so. If they refuse to grow up, it may be that they cannot get a handle on the satisfaction and self-definitions which come from that role.

In a recent article reviewing research in the field, a thoughtful social scientist made the following observations:

> Child-rearing is no longer a reliable source of personal meaning. In this post-modern era, adolescent children may damage rather than enhance their parents' self-esteem by repudiating their central values. Further erosion of parental authority, if it should occur, is likely to be accompanied by an increase in rejection by parents of adolescents; adults may well abandon their parental role earlier in the life cycle. The reduction of legal adult status to age eighteen may be a first important step designed to liberate parents from their children. [Diana Baumrind, "Early Socialization and Adolescent Competence," in *Adolescence in the Life Cycle,* ed. Sigmund E. Dragastin and Glen H. Elder, Jr. (New York: John Wiley and Sons, 1975), 139-140.]

Who is rejecting whom? And where do we find anything in this statement about the satisfactions of parenthood and adulthood? Parenting is reduced to hardships from which one seeks liberation. In what traditional system were parents promised "personal meaning" from children? The role of parents is in part to transmit meaning to children, to help them discover legitimate sources of personal meaning. No child can make a parent's life meaningful if the parent has not in his own search for meaning discovered the traditional and committing role of parent to be one crucial source of that meaning.

This quotation seems to me to be looking for a rationalization for parents' abandoning the parent role and their children. Are children really rejecting parents' values and authority, or are they rather expressing and giving behavioral form to the parents' lack of commitment and individual self-seeking?

The task for all societies and all parents is to present an image of adulthood which attracts the young and makes the struggle to grow up worth it. Can we develop for our young some such model?

One interesting development over the last ten to fifteen years has been the remarkable turn of the young toward the very old. Beginning with the hippies but continuing on, the youth culture has developed a significant respect for really old people. Old men who, for years, had wandered on our campus with complete anonymity are now approached and engaged in conversation. Young students in graduate school decided that their real interest in socialization and development lay in the upper reaches of age distribution, not in early childhood. Jessamyn West's story, "Sixteen"—about a young woman's growth in response to her grandfather's imminent death—became a favorite. Gutman theorized that contemporary youth were in many respects psychologically like the very old. *Harold and Maude* became an underground film classic.

What I make of this affinity is another sign of the muddy and ambiguous picture we have of adulthood. The young look to the very old as perhaps the right consultants about adulthood. After all, the old have successfully navigated the period. Perhaps the young are looking for a definition of adulthood with which they can identify.

Returning now to the adolescent in the family, how can we support youngsters and their parents, teachers, and community leaders [in their efforts] to understand each other better and to use their interrelation for more effective growth?

On the basis of clinical work and the experience of watching my friends and my own family go through adolescent growth, I think that, most of all, adolescents need contact with satisfied and effective adults, both inside and outside the family. And sometimes the parent-child relationship needs an intervening third person who can mediate and interpret the parties to each other.

To the extent that the adolescent enjoys positive and relatively nonevaluative friendships with young adults, his capacity for empathy and taking the role of the other will grow to include relationships with adults, even perhaps the parents. Friendship with young adults will also offer the adolescent other models of adulthood with which he can identify.

And any setting that allows interaction between adolescents and adults around a real problem or task is most likely to stimulate the growth of genuine friendship between age groups.

Adolescents are well defended against adults' overt efforts to influence or mold them. They are likely also to be defensive toward parents and teachers. On the other hand, teachers who allow youngsters a glimpse of themselves outside the role of teacher, and adult coworkers, bosses, and acquaintances—if these people are also gratified adults—can offer models to the young and significantly influence the directions they take.

6. Education and the State: Learning Community

Joseph Schwab

THE HEART OF THE MATTER

There is double meaning in the subtitle of this chapter. First, community can be learned. Community is not primarily a matter of place, of village, or of small town. It is a body of propensities toward action and feeling; propensities that, once acquired, can be expressed in many social circumstances.

Second, learning—human learning, at any rate—is a communal enterprise. Where the learning is knowledge, that knowledge is garnered by a community of which we are only the most recent members, and it is conveyed by word and gesture devised, preserved, and passed on to us by that community. Where the learning is development of latent capabilities, the first attempts to develop latent competencies are undertaken only with the encouragement and support of members of the community. Potential is further developed only through imitation and collaboration made possible by members of that community. Even "experience" as a form of learning becomes experience only as it is shared and given meaning by transactions with fellow human beings.

These two meanings of "learning community" meet, in practice, to

This chapter is drawn from a volume prepared with the support of the National Science Foundation, Grant No. ERP 7307947 AO 3. Any opinions, findings, conclusions, or recommendations expressed are those of the author and do not necessarily reflect the views of the National Science Foundation.

constitute one whole. The propensities that constitute community are learned only as we act and interact with others to develop processes through which other learnings take place. Meanwhile, the support, communication, and example that make possible these other learnings become accessible and acceptable only as the propensities toward community develop.

Although communal propensities, once developed, can find expression in many social circumstances, they do not develop in any social circumstance. They require rewarding collaboration, communication, helping, and being helped toward goals that we have set ourselves or that have been set for us by need and want. Among these goals, learning stands high, and, for the young, learning stands high indeed. ("All men by nature desire to know," say scholars as far apart in time and interest as Aristotle and Jean Piaget.) It follows, then, that a school, in some sense and form, should constitute the social climate in which the propensities toward community can develop. The American public school can become such a school.

The two meanings of "learning community," and their practical union in the public schools, are integral to an understanding of this chapter, and six points encompass the span of the argument.

COMMUNITY

Since the propensities that constitute community are propensities toward action and feeling and concern the relations of persons, anecdote rather than exposition is best suited to introducing the character of community.

When I was nine or ten years old, I ran away from home—all of twenty-five miles—to the next Mississippi town. Off the freight train, shakey and scared, I was sitting on the porch steps of an old-fashioned, frame hotel near the railway station to catch my breath when I noticed a man's legs beside me. I looked up and saw an ordinary, biggish man from the country, from a farm. He was sunburned and hardhanded, with skin dead white where his hat usually covered his head (at that moment, the hat was pushed loosely back).

After we greeted each other, he said, "I'm alone and fixing to eat a bite. Want to keep me company? It's on me."

After two or three seconds hesitation, I agreed, and we started walking toward the corner. Then he stopped, looked down, and grunted. When I looked up, he explained, "My shoe's untied, and my back has a crick in it. Would you mind?" I knelt down and tied his shoe.

Around the corner we entered a cafe and sat down side by side at the counter. I ordered an egg sandwich and a coke, and he followed my lead.

As we ate, he talked about why he was in town, and about his house and crops. He asked whether I had a garden.

I told him some things about my garden. At one point he said, "Hey, that's a good idea." At other points, he talked about ways to care for gardens that were different from mine.

Then he asked what else I did besides gardening and going to school, and I told him that I read books. He said he didn't read much, and no books at all. He asked what it was like to read books, and I tried to tell him.

When the food was gone, he asked, "You're not from here, are you?"

"No," I replied, "I'm from Columbus."

"I only asked," he informed me, "because there's a train headed south from here in about ten minutes." There was a short silence. Then, "You want to go home?"

I thought about it two or three seconds. Then I said, "Yes."

At that, he pulled a dollar bill from his pocket and said, "For carfare. You can pay me back sometime."

I got off the stool and started to leave. When I reached the door, I looked back. He was swishing the ice around in his glass and looking at it. I never learned his name.

Some parts of community in that episode are obvious: the man's impulse to be helpful, yielding to the impulse instead of dismissing it, giving the time (and the dollar) it took to be helpful.

But much of community lies hidden in other parts of the encounter—and in some of its silences. One instance is revealed in the first words the man spoke after our greeting ("I'm alone . . . ."). I was alone, too, and feeling it. He knew that, but did not mention it, for that would have humbled me, made me an inferior receiving a favor. Instead, he made us equals—not, of course, by making himself a child or by pretending I was an adult, but by making me a person fit to be company for a man.

He reinforced that contribution to my selfhood by asking help in tying his shoe. He knew that community includes giving. This is especially important for children since they are too often receivers, too rarely givers, of help. To give is to be useful, a sign of selfhood to the giving self, an assurance of earned membership, not merely membership conferred.

Still another aspect of community lies in symbolic collaboration as we talked together of farm and garden: his getting an idea from me and saying so; his suggesting ideas to me.

In the exchange about reading books, he sought a difference between him and me, and, when he found it, he honored it. Because I was different, I was interesting—not suspect or feared or held in contempt.

Another subtle sign of community lay in his not looking after me as I went to the door. No watching to see whether I would do as I should. Just an indication that we had had a moment of community that was now over.

Of course, it was not over. He had satisfaction from his gift to me, and that satisfaction meant that, on another occasion, he would give again. As for me, I got a small glimpse of what I had left home to find. I have not forgotten.

The elements of community suggested here (helping and being helped; collaboration; a relation, not merely of roles or ranks, but of persons; honoring of difference; accrual to selfhood, muting of authority) are only some of the elements. Community operates on a front that is much broader than face-to-face encounter. Nevertheless, the anecdote and its elements suffice as a sketch of what is involved in community conceived as propensities and as the acts that issue from propensities.

Why Does Community Matter?

The value and importance of community lie in its contribution to three distinct but related factors. It is indispensable to the development of individuality. It is also necessary for the maintenance of the social and political structure—the organization of duties, privileges, and operations through which people live in relative peace with one another and solve the problems (ecologic, demographic, economic) that affect and involve us all. Finally, it is essential to satisfying conviviality, that interplay of persons as persons without which the existence of men as social animals is barren.

Consider, first, the cherished matter of selfhood, identity, individuality. Contrary to the popular sociology that opposes individual and society, individuality can arise only in society, only through community. Individuality is not a genetic given, growing of itself and merely awaiting discovery. It must be developed.

Development begins in childhood, in the initial trial of possible capabilities. The incipient self, however, because it is merely incipient, cannot confidently identify its potential. It requires reassurance from more complete, other selves. Hence, individuality begins from a double germ—not merely self-recognition of potential, but communal recognition as well.

Continued development of individuality, as well as its initiation, requires community. We test our growing capabilities by affecting others through them and noting the responses of others to our acts. Courage to explore new possibilities is given by the example of others' explorations and by their response to our own efforts and successes.

Identity, in brief, is not discovered by introspection, but created by the slow accretion and ultimate crystallization of character through involvement with others, involvement in problems, involvement with the elements of culture. Individuality forms only in continuous interplay—community—with the persons and situations in which it comes to be.

The role of community in the maintenance of social and political structure is often obscured by the surface content of theories of society and polity. The patent content of most of these theories, even those concerned with polity and society as means for enrichment of human life, concerns the need for system, law, contract, exchange of goods, negotiation, persuasion and assent, sensibility, intellectual operations of various sorts, and management of conflict. These are the matters, at any rate, that are discussed by most of those who discuss or remodel such theories. A fresh study of these theories, however, shows that the effective operation of systems, laws, and techniques depend in whole or in part on an underlying community, or draw additional effectiveness from the operation of community.

John Dewey's conception of "The" public and its management is a minimal case in point. In summary paraphrase, he says, in *The Public and Its Problems:*

> We take our starting points from the objective fact that human acts have consequences upon others, from the fact that some of these are perceived and that their perception leads to efforts to control action so as to obtain some consequences and avoid others. The consequences are of two kinds, those which affect mainly the persons who act and those which affect others as well. In this difference we find the germ of the distinction between the public and the private [12]. The line between them is drawn on the basis of the extent and scope of consequences so important as to need control. The public consists of those who are so affected by the indirect consequences that it is deemed necessary to take systematic steps to control them. Officials are agents who look out for and take care of the interests thus affected [16], and undertake control of the behaviors which generate or avert extensive and enduring results of weal and woe [19]. A public is organized in and through those agents who act on behalf of its interests [28].[1]

On the surface, then, we have organizations (publics, "The" public, agencies) and their actions (formation of publics, "appointment" of agents, notice and control of publics, interests and actions by agents). But what is it that forms and maintains an effective public? What enables publics to select agents and confer on them the power to negotiate in their interest? What permits negotiation to reach decision? What constrains various publics to act in fulfillment of the decisions of their agents?

The quick and vulgarly "pragmatic" answer to most of these questions is self-interest evinced in a process of threat, counterthreat, and trade-off. Bestowal of power on agents, for example, is accompanied by the threat of withdrawal of power, should the agent fail to please his constituency. Publics form in response to recognition of a common material interest and the need to protect it. Publics fulfill decisions of agents lest failure to do so result in reprisal by other publics.

Such "pragmatic" threats and trade-offs undoubtedly contribute to the functioning of such a system, but is their effect sufficient to account for the system's operation—in those instances where the system functions effectively enough to bring publics and "The" public (that is, integration of publics into an effective whole) into existence, and agents continue to act in the interest of their publics and not in the interest of the conclave of agents (bureaucracy)?

Numerous counterinstances suggest that the answer is "No." The Metternichean influence in international relations which involves threat, counterthreat, and bargaining, is regularly punctuated by war as the mark of its failure. Regulatory agencies remote from those whose interest they were intended to serve, but in frequent touch with those to be regulated, move soon and often to serve their own interests and the interests of the regulated.

Certain time intervals in the process supply another indication that the answer is "No." When agents finally reach a decision, there comes a time when they separate to report to their constituents (union agents to their membership, a corporation's agent to its directors). Each agent trusts other agents to make a reasonably fair report, though profit can often accrue to the agent who falsifies at the expense of other agents. The union membership, when it votes to approve its agent's recommendation, even though that recommendation confers less than they had hoped or expected, again exhibits trust. Trust operates again when the voting members honor their vote by returning to their jobs; and, again, when corporate management honors the contract. (There is, of course, some threat involved.)

That community as well as power is involved in the effective working of the Deweyan structure is recognized by Dewey. He says, "Till the Great Society is converted into a Great Community, the Public will remain in eclipse."[2]

So much, then, for the importance of community to social-political structure and to individuality. Its contribution to satisfying conviviality goes almost without saying. Mere time passing, labor, and trade with others do not constitute a satisfying social existence. Some degree of community, of actualized recognition of others as parts of one's self and the corresponding recognition of one's self by others, is required. We emphasize, however, that the others need not be the same others time after time; nor need they be our geographic neighbors. The acts of recognition may be distributed among those different others with whom we trade, or labor, or pass time. They may be transactions in still other contexts: the line checking out at the supermarket; the fellow traveler; the next-door neighbor, transient though he may be; and, of course, the distant friend.

The very names for elements of the actualized recognition of others are enough to evoke a sense of their value: collaboration; the sharing of gaiety and sadness, of solace and joy, of disappointment and fulfillment; the giving and receiving of help; and, above all, communication of one's personal interpretations and valuings of the world.

The Withering of Community

Community, it would appear, is threatened with extinction in America. Our work involves others, but the others, on the whole, are considered competitors or henchmen, superiors or subordinates; they are not considered fellow human beings. We play with others—golf, tennis, bridge—but we play with mere cronies, men and women who like the same game, play at the right level of competence, and have the right day or evening free. They are not persons to us, nor we to them. If one dies or moves away, we find another to take his place. If we die or move away, we are easily replaced. Nothing much changes but the name.

Even the love we profess toward our children tends to contain less and less of community. We want, we say, to give them "every advantage." But every advantage is too often only what money will buy: clothes and toys, education, automobiles, summer camps, and travel. We employ professionals—coaches, therapists, teachers, counselors, even "play" directors—to provide professionalized substitutes for the transgenerational community that was once our children's birthright.

The story is much the same at the political-economic level. In the face of problems (inflation, energy shortages, pollution, unemployment, and others) that affect us all and require contribution from each of us toward their solution, we proffer not contribution toward solution but exacerbation of the problem. Labor union, management, and middlemen—each seeks mitigation of inflationary pains at the expense of the other two. Dense cities are encircled by chains of restrictive zonings while cities spoil the air and suburbs spoil the water of their neighbors.

Threats to Community

Community has been withered in America by the operation of four factors: social mobility, geographic mobility, the vast expansion of urban existence, and systematic inculcation of limits to community.

Among these threats, social mobility is probably the most potent and the most insidious. It is insidious because of the innocent face it wears. We see it as only a phase of social dynamics, as a matter of mild pride, or as both.

Many of us know, at first or second hand, the saga of early immigrants to America: their departure from poverty and oppression to find freedom and a job; the scrimping and saving to provide schooling for their children; the child's mastery of American ways and entry into a relatively secure and rewarding American economic role. Still more of us know the movement of the third generation to a life of greater security, more leisure, amenities. These forms of social mobility come easily to mind, and we are rightfully proud of them. To this pride we add pride in achievement and praise for the competitive spirit.

There is, however, a darker side to social mobility. In the first place, its earliest forms are accompanied by anxious sensitivity to expectations and grim conformity to them. We swallow our impulses to rebel and suppress our resentment of authority. These suppressions exact a price. Deference to authority becomes a habit, and we come to exact the same from subordinates. There can be no community with those we dominate or with those to whom we defer.

The competitive spirit, and achievement, undergo, in many of us, a similar passage from the praiseworthy to the destructive. The competitive spirit, which begins in emulation and the marshaling of energies, ends in a compulsive need to acquire at the competitor's expense. He is not bested but worsted. The sense of achievement which begins in aspiration to meet standards of excellence becomes the compulsion to outdo others and to be recognized as having outdone them. Hence, where first mobility tends to cut us off from superiors and subordinates, achievement and competition tend to cut us off from our peers.

Geographic mobility works in a less frightening way. Moves to a better house, a more fashionable suburb, or another city chop our life into episodes, and we permit that episodic life to interrupt community because we mistake *a* community—one familiar, small group of people—for community itself.

One important facet of community is a case in point: celebration. The loss of celebration among Americans, and Western peoples generally, has gone so far that most of us have forgotten what celebration means as a source and expression of community. It is the sharing of memories: remembrances of crises surmounted, defeats survived, triumphs shared among a kinship conferred by common roots and perpetuated by a shared style of life and value.

Such celebration, reenactment through drama and ritual, is one of the most potent expressions and preservers of community. Yet, to a great extent, only the dramas and rituals remain. We know what to do, say, and expect at Thanksgiving, Independence Day, the Mass, and the Seder meal, but we forget what the rituals celebrate. We forget because we expect remembered faces among the celebrants to remind us of the significance, and mobility has removed the remembered faces.

Urbanism, too, has withered community, even while conferring great advantages. Urbanism makes possible rich resources of intellect and sensibility: art and literature, music and drama, conversation and mutual challenge among good minds possessing much knowledge. But urbanism also exacts a price. One price is anonymity. We rarely even know who lives next door. Another is the activation of fear and suspicion of those who are different, especially fear and suspicion that others fear and suspect us. Activation comes about because those who are different walk the same streets and live on the same or a neighboring block. Anonymity alone would not wither community unless we conceived that community was limited to already familiar persons, but coupling anonymity with fear and suspicion makes anonymity hard to overcome.

Finally, the ugliest factor: our systematic inculcation of limits to community. A small group of real or alleged characteristics are effective triggers of ethnic-social class prejudice when conveyed to the young: stupidity, dishonesty, laziness, odor, lack of initiative, the "wrong" or odious diet. Odor and odious diet are effective triggers because we are easily conditioned to repugnance toward unfamiliar odors and foods. Because stupidity, laziness, and lack of initiative are ambiguous and hard to identify, this renders them apparently visible where we are taught to expect them. Fear of "dishonesty" is easily evoked by evident expectation of it, and evident expectation excludes the suspected from our moral community and leads the suspect to exclude us in turn.

Systematic conveyance of these triggers from generation to generation is ubiquitous in America, though the group to which they are attached *(and* the group which attaches them) varies from region to region and from time to time. Conspicuous targets include Blacks, Chicanos, American Indians, itinerant salesmen, blue-collar workers, Hungarians, Poles, Jews, Irish, and, not so long ago, "servants" and storekeepers. In virtually every region in America, the members of some groups are excluded from community with members of some other.

Concerning Revival of Community

These remarks about mobilities, urbanism, and prejudice are not just virtual truisms; three of them are truths about massive, inert conditions of modern life we can hardly hope to change. Only the very young or the very romantic can believe that we can reconstitute durable, small geographic communities on a useful scale. Some competitiveness and achievement orientation will, and probably should, continue to characterize much of our adult life. The city is here to stay. Policies of slow growth or no growth are likely, indeed, to worsen rather than better the condition of city populations. The inculcation of ethnic, national, social-class prejudice is another matter. There is a distinct possibility that an altered climate of the schools might constitute an effective counterforce to the inculcation of prejudice.

Even though we probably cannot erase urbanism and mobilities, we are not, with respect to community, doomed to the counsel of despair that would exist if community could arise *only* from the small, transgenerational, durable, face-to-face community (village, small town, extended family) that urbanity and mobility have destroyed. These face-to-face communities were, indeed, superb devices for instilling community, but they were by no means ideal, nor uniformly successful. They often failed, especially with the young who felt alien to and threatened by them. Boy or girl, the young adolescent felt himself a ward, a subordinate, clay being forced and molded into patterns of behavior with no place to hide, no place in which to experiment with alternative patterns of feeling and behavior. Because the young person felt unable to become himself, unable to feel he was a member of any community, he often had to leave the face-to-face community, to go away from the village and the extended family in search of community. He went, in fact, to the city.

This frequent failure of face-to-face community teaches us two lessons. First, the most important, it shows us that community is not necessarily a matter of place, of geography. *A* community and "community" are separable, different things. *A* community, in the ordinary sense, is a group of people who know each other by name and face (and history)—who frequently meet. But "community" is a state or condition of persons, a set of internalized propensities, of tendencies to feel and act in certain ways with other people. It is a condition of mind and heart that overflows into action and reaction. It may or may not characterize *a* community.

The second lesson taught us by the frequent failure of town and village is that community may conceivably be renewed by other means in other social structures, and be capable of expression in other social structures—even cities and suburbs, offices and factories, where populations are relatively transient.

What we now know of human behavior, its origins, and the factors that shape it tells us that what might be is, indeed, possible. The cluster of propensities toward action and passion, impulse, transaction, and response with respect to others, which we call community, can, indeed, be internalized, that is, made discoverable to the young, found desirable by them, and clothed in patterns of behavior and language appropriate to their expression. This is a constellation of factors that constitute community and of means by which they can be internalized without coercion or parochial indoctrination.

The Public School as the Place for Revival of Community

If there is to be revival of American community, it requires an institution that is American, a place open to all and receiving all, cutting across and including the numerous economic, social, ethnic, and religious groups that constitute us. The alternative is numerous closed communities at odds with one another. The tax-supported school is the American institution that comes closest to being such a place and the one that shows the greatest promise of closing the remaining gap between fact and promise.

These remarks about an American place do not signal a proposed revival of a melting pot policy. That policy, in the early years of this century, sought to destroy the supportive standards and styles that immigrants brought with them in the alleged interest of patriotism and of fitting the immigrant to his new surroundings and enabling him to get ahead. We, on the other hand, propose maintenance of supportive differences. The principal reason why it should be an American place is to provide nourishing occasions and circumstances for discovery by children that the differences among them arising from membership in different intermediary groups (ethnic, social-class, or another) are rewarding, not threatening. This will, of course, require design of classroom situations in which differences do, in fact, add interest to classroom activities, contribute to successful learning by each child, and are preserved.

The tax-supported public school may be, in the abstract, the most appropriate institution for revival of community, but two questions about its use remain: Does the American tradition of hegemony of the home over moral instruction (and any attempt at revival of community is moral instruction) permit or should it permit an effective role for the schools in this regard? Are schools in a position to take on this burden in addition to those they now carry?

One factor contributes toward answering both of these questions. The sociologist, C. Arnold Anderson, tells us that procedures of the classroom, the manner in which teaching occurs, attitudes of teachers toward children, conditions imposed by way of approval or disapproval, models afforded by individuals' expressed attitudes toward one another and toward school authority, and the very pattern of school lessons have been shown to be effective instruments of moral instruction.[3] Ralph Tyler, one of America's most able and experienced educators, informs us of studies showing that the social and political attitudes of persons from a similar educational background in small Georgia towns and in New York City were more alike than the attitudes of fellow New Yorkers (or fellow Georgians) with different schooling.[4]

Schools, then, are agencies of moral instruction, of internalization—instruction and internalization that occur not through explicitly directed units of curriculum but through the teacher-student relationship and the social-psychological climate of the classroom. It follows that revival of community would constitute no additional burden to the schools. It would not be achieved by additions or changes in the substance of curriculum, but, rather, by modification of the climate of instruction and the patterns of school lessons.

As to the tension between home and school as agencies of moral instruction, the conditions cited by Anderson and Tyler show that it is, indeed, a tension, not a dichotomy. School, as well as the home, contributes to the attitudes and values of children. The models afforded by parents vie (in part) with the models afforded by the teacher, by other children, and by the characters of fiction and history that the school makes accessible to children. The relations of child and adult in the home and the relations of children to one another and to the adults of the schoolroom are similar in some respects, different in others. Home as well as school teaches "lessons," but the patterns of these lessons differ. To suggest, then, that schools consciously and conscientiously adapt their power to affect attitudes and values toward enhancement of community does not constitute invasion of a de facto exclusive privilege of the home.

There is no doubt that the moral force of homes, taken alone, is, in many instances and respects, a centrifugal one. Home differs from home. They are divided by ethnicities, national origins, religious and social-class differences. The moral force of the school, on the other hand, would be centripetal. It is precisely this balance between the centrifugal and the centripetal that is needed.

The centripetal tendency of the school, taken alone, would press us toward the bland homogeneity that the melting pot policy happily failed to achieve. Centripetal movement, alone, would deprive us of that diversity of alternative styles and values that is the cultural resource by which we meet changes in social problems and conditions, the cultural equivalent of the genetic diversity through which living species survive changes in the physical environment.

The centrifugal tendency of homes, on the other hand, would, alone, continue in many cases to generate fear and anxiety among those who differ in style and values—the same fears and anxieties that constitute one of the great barriers to community in America.

The two together, however—centripetal (school) and centrifugal (home)—should allow diversity of perspectives and propensity toward action. School balanced by home would yield an appreciation of the uses and advantages of diversity and permit communication and collaboration among the diverse. A communicating, collaborative diversity of perspectives and propensities would yield satisfactions in the very acts of communication and collaboration, as well as provide material advantages perceptible to those involved. Such satisfactions and advantages are the essential nutrients of community.

NOTES

1. This paraphrased summary is based on John Dewey, *The Public and Its Problems* (Chicago: Swallow Press, 1954). The bracketed numbers identify pages from this edition. The volume was originally published in 1927 by Henry Holt and Co., New York.

2. *Ibid.*, 142.

3. See, for example, C. Arnold Anderson, "Education and Society," in *International Encyclopedia of the Social Sciences,* Volume 4 (New York: Macmillan Co. and the Free Press, 1968), 518b.

4. Personal communication at a conference on education held in Chicago, November 1973.

PART TWO
Transition to the World of Work

7. Education, Jobs, and Community Services: What Directions for National Policies?

Stephen K. Bailey

During the Second World War, I was for some time the only American officer on the island of Cyprus. I developed a considerable interest in that tiny, tragic, conflict-ridden territory. In the late 1950s, when the fragile Cypriot peace dissolved into violence, I found myself in London having lunch with Britain's leading specialist in that area. We discussed old times, and, finally, I asked him the ultimate question: What is the solution? He looked at me with that wonderful combination of compassion and disdain that Sons of the Empire reserved in those days for callow American pretenders to the mantle of world leadership and said, "Bailey, old boy, the trouble with you Americans is that you believe that if there is a problem, there is a solution."

These discussions of the youth problem remind me of this important lesson in intellectual maturity. If there is a youth problem in the United States, it may well be that there is no practical solution. Costs; structural rigidities of the labor market; the supervisory, pedagogic, and administrative burdens of carrying out relevant public policies; unacceptable social and economic trade-offs, such as inflation, job demands associated with the women's liberation movement, the prospect that more heads of families will be unemployed, increased competition with the elderly for jobs; the reluctance of youth themselves

---

Paper presented to the ICED-Aspen Seminar Program, July 30, 1976, Aspen, Colorado.

"to be done good to at"; the disruption of recruiting pools for the armed services—these and other possible consequences and constraints may militate against any concerted effort to right observable wrongs.

To complicate matters even further, however, it is not at all clear what wrongs are in fact observable—what the "problem of youth" really is. Many may remember the final minutes of the life of Gertrude Stein. "What is the answer?" she asked her lifelong friend, Alice B. Toklas. Alice replied, "There is no answer." "What then," asked Gertrude, with her last breath, "is the question?"

Clark Kerr has brilliantly exposed the youth problem disaggregated into its myriad diversities, concocting some heuristic social geometry to illuminate recurring tendencies in human development and in the social expectations of a capitalistic democracy like the United States. The geometry helped to reconstruct some general problems that the disaggregation had already dispersed. But Kerr was the first to suggest that the realities behind the geometry were more complicated than the geometry itself. And so they are. Americans no longer look at education as something that takes place between ages six and twenty-four. The average age of Americans attending community colleges this year is twenty-nine, which means that many citizens above the age of twenty-nine are enrolled in community college courses. Millions of preschool children in America are in nursery schools, or in day-care centers that have at least some educative components.

Looking at the adolescent and young adult years of, say, fourteen to twenty-four, most American youngsters have a fairly elaborate set of options involving combinations of education, peer-oriented recreation, and job experience. They perform such tasks as delivering newspapers, baby-sitting, short-order cooking in fast-food establishments, soda jerking in ice cream parlors, car washing, performing unskilled tasks in restaurants, working on highway jobs in the summers, doing yard work for neighbors. In the education field, high schools provide educational opportunities, at least through age sixteen. Postsecondary education offers a real option for millions of young people. Within a single decade the number of enrollments in our more than 3,000 colleges and universities has doubled from 5.5 million in 1965 to 11.2 million in 1975. There are at least 12,000 proprietary schools in America serving additional millions of young people. And postsecondary education is available to far more than the rich. Federal public assistance in the form of student aid, loans, and work-study programs presently helps 2.3 million students. And this figure does not include the 750,000 students aided through the family assistance program of social security or the million students benefiting from veterans' educational allowances. Nor does it include student aid made available through the treasuries of state governments and through the philanthropic and internal resources of private colleges and universities. Many students in the United States do not pay the "sticker price" for their education. And, except in proprietary schools, even the "sticker price" rarely represents the total cost.

It has been argued that we have artificially separated youth and young adults from intergenerational contacts. But this is only partly true, and, in many cases where peer contacts have been reinforced at the expense of intergenerational contacts, the experience has been highly liberating. In personal terms, most tyrannizing in human history has been suffered in the intrafamily experience. And it would, I think, be a mistake to romanticize apprenticeships. They can smooth the path to adult occupations, but the pains—sometimes even cruelties and indignities—of the apprenticeship system did not begin or end with Charles Dickens.

On the general subsistence front, family support, welfare payments, food stamps, intermittent jobs combined with unemployment compensation, work-study, student aid, and an increasing variety of state and federal work-relief and job-training programs mitigate real hardship for the overwhelming majority of those young people who do not have steady employment. American youth, like all youth, bump along with the normal anxieties of adolescence, but few starve, and most of them have almost endless activity options—wine, music, sex, TV, radio, records, tapes, automobiles, motorcycles, sports, unsystematic wanderings, movies, education and training, ice cream parlors, magazines, beer parties, surfing, drugs, gangs, communes, the races. In the minds of many young people, serious responsibilities will come soon enough and will last a long time.

So the life of youth in America is only partly structured. For many it is highly libertarian. Why should a bunch of over-the-hill elders want to spoil the fun and the largely free ride? If the Chinese want to fill young lives with school, work, and patriotic ceremonials, that is their business. If the Germans want to subject large numbers of young people to the strictures and disciplines of apprenticeships, that is up to them. But if a wealthy country like the United States wants to indulge its young people with a smorgasbord of educational opportunities and libertarian recreation options in order to protect the adult labor market, provide quality of occupational opportunity for women and the elderly, and preserve the preconditions of a volunteer armed service, why shouldn't it? Does not youth's very resilience make this the age cohort most able to bear the uncertainties and disutilities of a soft labor market?

In what I have just described, I have not intended to set up a straw man. Eighteen-year-olds can vote. If the eighteen to twenty-four-year-old cohort were massively discontented, they could have organized a political campaign in recent years that would have brought our political leaders to their knees. They have not. In fact, few vote at all. What, then, is the problem, or, in Gertrude Stein's idiom, what are the questions? Surely the issue is not that youth behavior is an affront to the mores of the older generation. In a free society, it is the business of youth to be unsettling to their elders. Otherwise, who would maintain the phalanxes of irreverence needed to conquer the bastions of tradition? Not all newness, of course, is liberating, but then neither is all tradition.

There are, it seems to me, five things wrong with settling for such a scenario in terms of American youth. First of all, it is a distorted picture of reality. There are massive injustices in the present system. As Clark Kerr noted, for some older adolescents or young adults—those from upper-middle-class homes—unemployment may be only 3 percent. In some urban ghettos the unemployment rate for the same age group may be 70 to 80 percent. Mobility and educational attainment in this nation is still closely linked to family income. Three-quarters of American youth never graduate from college. In addition, the poor cannot afford many of the recreational options that delight the wandering youth representative of the more affluent segments of society. Vast numbers of young people are locked into locations and situations from which there are no easy escapes and which provide little sense of excitement about either the present or the future because of the lack of purposeful activity options and because of the limiting and unchallenging nature of even those jobs that are available. In spite of recent progress, only a limited number of women and minorities are in the educational pipeline that will ensure a decent chance at the brass rings of higher status in the society. The inequalities of youth tend to be perpetuated in the patterns of adult life.

This scenario also ignores the extent of psychological disintegration that is manifest in large segments of American youth, affluent as well as poor: drugs, alcohol, violence, drifting, loneliness, manifest alienation. Major crimes of violence are largely perpetrated on society by young people. Disrespect for property in the form of vandalism, shoplifting, and larceny is endemic. Experiments for kicks often reach the demonic and the sadistic. Suicide among young people is increasing. Many sense a fundamental uselessness and purposelessness in their lives as society communicates to them the idea that they are not really essential or even wanted. In a study of American youth sponsored by the American Council on Education in the 1930s, Dorothy Canfield Fisher noted that: "The sense of uselessness is the severest shock which the human system can sustain."

Yet a third thing mars the scenario. The superfluity of youth could well turn our all-volunteer armed services into a potentially dangerous professional military establishment. When the military becomes an occupational model, as it has, and employment opportunities in the general economy are limited, those young people who initially enlisted voluntarily tend to reenlist. This erodes the notion that military service should be supplied by civilians whose basic orientation is not military, and it could mean that the military will ultimately be made up of professionals who started as volunteers but who subsequently lost all sense of identity with the civilian polity. Youth faced with limited opportunity tends to exacerbate this dangerous tendency.

The United States has accumulated a vast horde of unmet social needs: adequate care of the elderly and the handicapped; health services, especially for the poor and in rural areas; environmental improvement; educational services for the deprived and the disadvantaged; welfare and recreational services of all kinds; urban redevelopment; and many more. And it is these needs that further mar the scenario. Don Eberly reports that, in 1965, Greenleigh Associates estimated a need for 4.5 million jobs in the United States, mostly in education and health, for persons with few preentry skills. He also points out that, in the same year, the National Commission on Technology, Automation, and Economic Progress reported a need for 5.3 million subprofessional people working in the fields of health, education, beautification, welfare, urban development, and public protection. Probably 400,000 man-years of effort are needed to meet the conservation needs associated with maintaining our cultural life: public libraries, churches and synagogues, museums, the performing arts, botanical gardens, zoos, parks, playgrounds. Many of these lack adequate financial support and have become sorely dilapidated and understaffed. With all of these unmet social needs, it is a kind of madness not to harness the energies of underemployed, underutilized young people in an effort to overcome our patent social deficit.

The fifth, and, from my point of view, most serious thing wrong with the scenario is that unemployed and underemployed youth who stay alive solely from family and public handouts begin to lose all sense of social responsibility. There is a quotation from Edward Gibbon that reads in part: "When the Athenians finally wanted not to give to society but for society to give to them, when the freedom they wished for most was freedom from responsibility, then Athens ceased to be free." We do not know what prolonged dependence will do to generations of American youth. But society takes a terrible risk when it decides not to involve its young in activities and decisions that constitute the essence of a responsible democratic polity.

We are by no means the first to worry about such matters. A seven-year study (1935-1942) by the American Youth Commission of the American Council on Education testifies to this. More than a score of studies dealing with all aspects of the youth problem were commissioned. One of these, Howard Bell's *Youth Tell Their Story,* published in 1938, became a minor sociological classic. It summarized and analyzed over 13,000 personal interviews with young people in the state of Maryland between the ages of sixteen and twenty-four. The first act passed in the dramatic first hundred days of Roosevelt's New Deal in 1933 authorized the Civilian Conservation Corps, which put young unemployed males to work in semimilitary camps devoted to conservation and to the renewal of natural resources. Later, the Federal Emergency Relief Administration and the Works Progress Administration developed job programs for unemployed youth. More significant, in terms of subsequent events, was the development of two programs under the National Youth Administration, the so-called "school-related jobs" and "out-of-school jobs for the young" programs.

World War II, of course, absorbed all of our national energies and especially the energies of young people. A predicted postwar depression did not in fact materialize, in part because the GI Bill constituted a cushioning policy for the nation. It increased enormously the stock of developed human resources in America and contributed mightily to the technological prowess of the United States in the 1950s and 1960s. One economist has estimated that the federal investment of billions of dollars in the GI Bill from 1946 to 1973 yielded a sixteenfold return—solely in terms of increased federal tax payments.

Reasonable full employment and enormously expanded secondary and higher education enrollments in the 1950s and 1960s gave most youth a sense of purposeful activity and of being needed and valued in the society. Perhaps the high point was reached in the early 1960s when the Peace Corps caught the idealism and imagination of millions of Americans. It had a peak enrollment of 15,000 persons. Even today it enrolls nearly 7,000 persons and has an annual budget of 80 million dollars.

Even so, young Spanish-speaking and black minorities did not share in the euphoria of the early 1960s. Unemployment for those living in urban ghettos was five to ten times higher than it was for suburban and rural middle-class youth. A part of President Johnson's Poverty Program (and subsequently a substantial number of other federal programs—alas, often overlapping, often competing with one another) was directed at the unemployment of young people from poor subcultures. Without going into detail, I mention a few titles: Job Corps; Neighborhood Youth Corps; College Work-Study Programs (including the so-called Urban Corps to place students in city agencies); VISTA (acronym for Volunteers in Service to America, which is a kind of domestic Peace Corps and currently enrolls 4,500 volunteers); and a variety of other volunteer programs under the auspices of the federal agency known as ACTION. Other programs include a University Year for ACTION, the Program for Local Service, as well as a series of nonyouth programs, including Foster Grandparents and a retired Service Volunteer Program.

Meanwhile, on the education front, there has been the development of career education programs to orient pupils and students to the world of work—cooperative education programs designed to interlard school experiences with actual work experiences encountered in industry. There have also been service learning schemes concocted but not yet implemented. Clark Kerr, Frank Newman, James Coleman, Willard Wirtz, and other luminaries have been ruminating, but nothing has yet materialized. In April 1976 I testified before the Democratic National Platform Committee on the need for a youth policy that would relate educational opportunities to jobs and to public service. And there was a Universal Youth Service Conference, sponsored by the Eleanor Roosevelt Institute and held at the Franklin D. Roosevelt Library in the same year. There have been at least fifteen related congressional bills introduced in the last five or six months. Adam Yarmolinsky prepared a thoughtful policy paper for President

Carter on the youth problem issue prior to his election. The Rand Corporation, under the leadership of Mike Timpane, has prepared a substantial paper for the office of the assistant secretary of HEW for planning and evaluation that is entitled *Youth, Policy, and Transition.* The paper questions the seriousness of the problem, at least as outlined by James Coleman, John Henry Martin, and Frank Brown in studies conducted in the early 1970s that followed the youth *Angst* of the late 1960s. In short, the issue, in one or more of its various manifestations, is very much alive politically.

Where in essence are we? What really is needed in the field of public policy? If we take seriously the five problems identified earlier, that is, inequality, psychological disintegration, the professionalization of the armed services, unmet social needs, and the loss of a sense of social responsibility, it seems clear that no one national youth policy can possibly be adequate. I cannot believe that a compulsory, universal, national service program, for example, would be politically or administratively feasible, or even desirable. Even if voluntary service programs are developed, I doubt that we can even come close to the military regimens that were associated with the CCC camps of the 1930s—any more than Germany in 1976 can revive the *Arbeitsdienst* of 1936. There is simply a change in cultural climate. Former Congressman Andrew Young was hooted down at the Universal Youth Service Conference when he suggested that youth be subject to disciplines associated with the military, even in civilian service roles. The fact is, however, that bits and pieces of public policy are, in John Gardner's phrase, lying all around needing to be put together.

Part of the problem *is* jobs, and unequal access to them. This problem will be demographically acute for at least another ten years, especially among the poor, the minorities, and the unskilled. Without structural changes in the economy, youth unemployment will, I believe, be a serious problem as far ahead as anyone can see, especially in urban centers. The government should offer incentives to industry to increase the hiring of young people, and the government should also promote public works and public service programs, using government funds to provide as many job opportunities as possible for young people. Although Congress may not pass the Hawkins—Humphrey full employment bill, I am confident that, within a year or so, something like it will be enacted that will provide for planning for youth employment and will delegate to local communities and states substantial responsibility for implementing such a policy.

Job programs for the poor alone will, however, divide young people into participants and nonparticipants, that is, those who do not need to participate. It is for this reason that I would like to see a work-study youth program that starts at the age of fourteen. Participants would be paid a minimum wage for a limited amount of public service each week. But only one-third of the wage would be paid in cash, at least until the participant reached the age of sixteen. The other two-thirds would be set aside to provide for future plans. At the age of sixteen, the participant could choose to take the full amount set aside in cash or one-half in cash and the remainder as an educational bonus equal to one and a half times the amount owed him. Young people ready for postsecondary education would receive a new form of student aid, besides already existing student aid provisions, that would allow postsecondary educational options, as well as a guaranteed access presently denied to many of the poor in this nation.

Low tuition policies at the state level, buttressed by student-aid packages at the federal level, should not make postsecondary education for a larger segment of young people just a holding tank until jobs become available; it should constitute a marvelous opportunity to develop personal and interpersonal skills, aesthetic skills, coping skills, hobby skills, public problem-solving skills, and voluntary service skills that will enrich all the days of their lives and set a pattern for lifelong learning. If jobs for many people are going to be dull and limiting and if we are going to have more leisure time, more time to ourselves, then one of the great functions of education is to provide people with the opportunity to learn skills and appreciations that can make a full and rich life outside of the paid job market.

For those who do not attend colleges and universities, I would submit that the National Endowment for the Arts and the Humanities, and other federal agencies should provide work-learning funds through libraries, museums, hospitals, recreation centers, and other cultural- and community-oriented agencies and instruments. On-the-job, released-time educational and training programs should be a part of all industrial, commercial, professional, governmental, and trade-union activity, and the cost should be shared by the federal government and by local entities. Local community work councils of the kind suggested by Willard Wirtz, with appropriate counseling staffs composed of educators, businessmen, labor or agricultural leaders, and local governmental and professional leaders, should, with federal support, become a familiar part of the social landscape of American life.

Educational institutions should become far more imaginative than they have been in the past in arranging to bring educational opportunities to young people on a dispersed, convenient basis and to adapt curricula to existing needs and not just the job needs of citizens, especially the young.

Military service should have a high educational component, now and in the future. Except in very special cases, service for any one enlistee should be limited to three years in order to preserve the civilian aspect.

Everything I have suggested, even if it were implemented tomorrow, would still be inadequate because the whole educational and employment system in this country cannot be divorced from health, welfare, and housing policies. To pretend that there are educational gimmicks that can eliminate the substructure of misery created by often counterproductive policies of government in such fields as health and welfare is to believe that the stork brings babies.

In the final chapter of *The Purposes of Education,* I make a recommendation that is particularly pertinent at the high school level and in large urban centers. It might also be a proposition for national experimentation: moving from a five- to a four-day educational week. Teachers would spend the fifth day in teacher centers similar to those found in Britain. Students would use the fifth day to move into the community in ways that would allow identity with adult peers in a variety of contexts: jobs, recreational activities, and special tutoring (able students tutoring slower students, grandmothers tutoring young people), among others. This might begin to knit the school and the students back into the larger community from which many have become alienated. It might give students what James Coleman calls an "action-rich" rather than just a "knowledge-rich" curriculum.

These seem to be some directions that public policy must take. *None of them is easy.* Experience indicates that all the barriers and rigidities and perversities identified earlier in this chapter are likely to endure. But the needs and dangers implicit and explicit in the existing situation are real. The individualism of American life, with all that it promises in the way of vitality and creativity, cannot exist forever without a social structure based upon increased social justice and an elemental and shared sense of community. Finally, I submit that personal and social integration are ultimately mirror images of one another.

8. More Youth Than Jobs

Robert J. Havighurst

According to . . . conventional wisdom, young people take a major solid step into adult identity by getting and holding a stable job. There are almost no other alternatives for boys. And girls are more and more achieving their initial adult identity through a job rather than through marriage.

If at any period in history boys in their late teens or early twenties have difficulty finding jobs, this is generally taken as a serious social and personal problem, predictive of alienation or political disturbances, and also of delinquency.

Since the numbers of young people reaching the age of eighteen amounted to four million for the first time in 1972 and will continue at this high level until 1979 after which there will be a rather sharp drop, it was to be expected that they might experience more difficulty getting into the adult labor force than their older siblings who reached their twenties during the 1960s when they were in smaller age cohorts.

This situation was worsened by the severe economic recession which came soon after 1972. The result is that in 1975–76 we have the highest rates of youth unemployment since the Depression decade of the 1930s, and possibly the current level of youth unemployment is greater than it was in the mid-1930s.

The relevant population facts are in Table 8-1. Even in the best of

Reprinted, with permission, from *The Center Magazine* 9 (May-June 1976): 16-19.

Table 8-1
Youth and the Working Force, 1960-2000

	Year					
Age group	1960	1970	1975	1980	1985	2000
			(millions)			
15-19	13.3	19.3	20.9	20.0	17.6	20.0 (est.)
20-24	10.8	17.2	19.3	21.2	20.3	19.8 (est.)
25-64	83.2	90.2	97.0	105.9	115.5	135.8
Total population, in millions	179	205	217	225	236	264 (est.)
Ratio between age groups						
15-19/25-64	.16	.21	.22	.19	.15	.15
20-24/25-64	.13	.19	.20	.20	.17	.15

economic conditions, the United States would have a problem of youth unemployment during the 1970s [owing] to the temporary very large birth cohorts of the 1950s. In 1975 we [had] 41 million young people between the ages of fifteen and twenty-four, compared with only 22 million in 1960. This group is about twice as large as the age group from fifty-five to sixty-five who are moving out of the labor force during this decade. In 1980 the situation will be equally difficult, with 41 million in the fifteen through twenty-four age group. After that, this age group will decrease in size, due to the relatively low birthrates since 1965. Thus, the youth unemployment problem is critical for the next ten years and may require temporary measures for this emergency period. Table 8-1 shows that the ratio of the fifteen through twenty-four age group to the twenty-five through sixty-four age group is about 50 percent higher for the period from 1970 to 1980 than it was in 1960.

The unemployment figures for young people have received less public attention recently than the unemployment levels of the twenty-five through sixty-four group, the men and women who have major responsibility for family support. However, the "official" unemployment data published by the Bureau of Labor Statistics state that the unemployment rate of youth (defined as the sixteen through nineteen age group) is three times as high as the rate for the total labor force. Furthermore, the actual unemployment rate of young people may be overestimated or underestimated by the BLS numbers because so many young people seek work only in the summer, and they spend a considerable amount of time looking for work, which marks them as "unemployed" at those times. On the other hand, many young people (and older ones as well) simply give up the search for work because they are convinced that it is useless to try to find a job. They do not register at an employment service office and therefore are not counted as unemployed. In any case, the BLS figures for 1973 showed the "unemployed" sixteen- through nineteen-year-olds to be 30 percent of the total unemployed group of all ages.

Unemployed young people are most numerous among the economically disadvantaged minority groups, especially the black and the Spanish origin groups. The official unemployment statistics are especially ambiguous for these groups. For example, the Chicago Urban League, early in 1975, estimated that about 50 percent of all black youth in Chicago aged sixteen through nineteen were unemployed.

The problem is now clearly visible and our society is worried; but no major solutions have been tried.

It seems clear that the conventional employers—private and public—cannot give work to all the youth in the age range sixteen through twenty-five who want it. The American economy simply does not have places for them and will not have places even if the [indexes] of economic activity get back to "normal." We cannot hope for a "natural solution" before 1985, when the age cohort born in 1961 will be twenty-four years of age, and will be followed by smaller cohorts, all with less than 4 million members.

There have been several quantitative analyses of this problem. It was pointed out by Kenneth Keniston in 1970. The Panel on Youth of the President's Science Advisory Council gave the problem wide publicity in 1973-74. . . . [In 1975 the National Society for the Study of Education published a yearbook entitled *Youth*] that gave major attention to it. The problem has been aired, but no constructive solutions have been established.

For obvious reasons, the public high school and community college have taken on a kind of custodial function for young people beyond the legal age of compulsory school attendance. No doubt a good many young people now attending senior high school or the first two years of college would have quit school and gone to full-time work if there had been jobs for them. Since 1970 the situation has somewhat stabilized, with 80 percent of an age cohort "graduating" from high school, 50 percent entering a postsecondary institution, and 25 percent completing a four-year college program.

The mid-1970s see the great majority of youth as politically quiet and oriented toward their own personal careers, in contrast to the general unrest of the mid-1960s. For example, the National Association of Secondary School Principals in 1974 published a report entitled *The Mood of American Youth: 1974,* based on a survey of a national sample of high school students made by the Gilbert Youth Research Corporation. Asked whether the high school is doing a good job of educating the respondent, 77 percent said "yes." Asked about their plans for the time after they leave high school, 47 percent said they would go to a two- or four-year college, and 12 percent to a vocational training school. Asked "to what degree does your high school give a good college preparatory program?" 18 percent said "very well," 45 percent said "adequately," 14 percent said "not very well or inadequately," and 23 percent said "no opinion."

Practically all high school students think that they should have some kind of employment. Only 8 percent said that high school students should not work or seek work, and 92 percent said they should be employed at least part-time. The favorite work program was a part-time, year-round job, favored by 84 percent of the high school students. Thus there is a wide gap between what high school students want in terms of employment and the actual employment facts for youth.

At this time, the next move is in the hands of the educators and the legislators. They have perhaps six types of solution from which to choose. These can be described as having either an economic or a humanistic emphasis. Also, they vary in the extent to which they depend on the public educational system for leadership and administration.

There are two possible time perspectives: One is focused on the next five years—the 1976–1980 period; The other is focused on the next twenty-five years—the 1976–2000 period.

For the 1976–1980 perspective, the emphasis is on helping young people to grow in maturity and socioeconomic competence while many of them are waiting to get into a stable and satisfactory occupational and family-centered career pattern. This perspective is based on the reasonable assumption that the American economy will make a strong and stable recovery, and that the labor force will absorb the products of the 1950–1960 baby boom fairly easily after 1980, when the oncoming young adult cohorts will be smaller.

For the 1976–2000 perspective, the emphasis is on helping young people understand the basic socioeconomic and value changes of American society which are now taking place, and to find their places, not only as workers and parents, but also as citizens of a society that is preparing itself for the twenty-first century. This perspective will require more attention to a high school and college curriculum which emphasizes problems of social values, social structure, and technology in a world which must solve its problems of population control, energy production, and conservation of essential minerals and chemicals so as to create a stable equilibrium for the twenty-first century.

The following descriptions of "models" illustrate the various alternatives that seem to be available:

1. A *national service corps* providing useful employment outside the private economy for about 2 million youths aged eighteen through twenty-four each year. If they were paid perhaps $2,000 a year for the socially valuable work they perform, the cost of the program would be about $4.5 million a year. The Congress will probably pass a bill to establish this kind of program within a year. This is reminiscent of the program of the National Youth Administration during the late 1930s. It might be administered through state youth authorities, which would have to be created in most of the states, there being only a few now in existence.

2. A *community service corps* carried on through community colleges and senior high schools, and administered by education agencies on a county or a city basis. This is an alternative to a National Service Corps, and would be administered by existing educational agencies. This would be most feasible in the big cities and in certain counties which have a county community college. Rural counties could work it out through the county school superintendent and the high school and community college directors in the county. Also, most big cities have such projects going on a small basis for youth who are out of school and out of work. These agencies could be brought together into some form of mobilization of resources for youth.

3. A program of *action learning* in senior high schools and community colleges, tied to the curriculum and providing graduation credit together with modest payment for students from low-income families. This differs from the preceding model mainly in the amount of emphasis on work for pay, as distinguished from emphasis on a variety of service activities where the service motive takes priority over the money-earning motive.

4. A program of *apprenticeship* in local business and industry. Employers—both private and public—would be asked to organize cadres of young workers to do useful jobs which do not reduce the em-

ployment of mature workers. This might be difficult to establish, though the present work-study programs in many cities could perhaps be expanded somewhat. However, these programs are generally geared to the needs of the employer to recruit new workers, and they have very little elasticity as far as numbers are concerned.

5. . . . Though this might be controversial, it would be possible to establish a number of subsistence-oriented *communes* on the edges of cities where young people could grow most of their food, keep a few cows and chickens, and perhaps draw simple clothing and food rations from a public supply station. There would be a number of controversial issues: How much adult supervision? How about coeducational communes? What kind of political ideologies might be encouraged or tolerated?

6. An *education for the future* program at senior high school and college levels for which selected students are given a cost-of-living stipend, while the majority are not subsidized. This has more of a humanistic than economic emphasis. It stresses a curriculum development that might catch on and become a central part of the liberal education of the sixteen- to twenty-year-olds of the next quarter century. Since it is aimed at all alert and intellectually able youth, regardless of their economic status, it should include a cost-of-living stipend for youth of low-income families, analogous to the Basic Educational Opportunity Grants which have been paid to college students from low-income families in recent years. The aim would be to help produce a socially sensitive and sophisticated group of college graduates who are prepared by their school and college studies to take the lead in fashioning the society of the year 2000, a society which will be prepared to meet the problems of human life on this planet in the twenty-first century.

This program might well begin in the senior year of high school, which needs curriculum options to make it come alive to the more ambitious students. The National Association of Secondary School Principals has called for optional courses in the twelfth grade to relieve what it calls the boredom of the one-track senior year program that prevails in most high schools. In its December 1975 *Curriculum Report,* the NASSP describes how a number of senior high schools are opening up the senior year curriculum, in cooperation with colleges which give college creadit for certain courses. Some of them are simply basic college freshman courses for which the high school senior gets college credit upon passing an examination. Others are experimental courses in which high school teachers and some of their students move into new areas where the main considerations are changing social values, problems of the relation of man to the natural environment, and problems of the relations between the developed and the underdeveloped parts of the world.

Possibly progress could be made with this kind of program through a joint curriculum commission funded by the National Endowment for the Humanities and the National Science Foundation.

The contemporary youth crisis calls for leadership and action by educators working at the high school and college levels. However, they will have to think and act outside of their accustomed routines. Youth need practical, maturity-promoting experience in the adult world, together with vision and perspective on the future of the society for which they will soon become responsible.

9. Problems of Youth in the Labor Market

Paul E. Barton

An intertwining of determinants of the youth employment condition makes it difficult, and not wholly useful, to speak only in traditional terms of what might constitute "labor market" factors. Recognizing the guilt that accompanies oversimplification, I would still like to suggest that the barriers to youth employment fall into the following categories: the shortage of jobs that accompanies a recession economy; the behaviors of key institutions that do not necessarily reflect "market" forces; the isolation of major institutions from each other, which impedes a smooth transition from school to work; the laws and institutional rules that create barriers; the inadequacies in information and lack of brokerage services that make labor markets operate inefficiently; and the shifts in the location of demand for youth labor.

These factors become interrelated. Laws may be extended in actual application because of institutional objectives and practices. Lack of information on the job market may contribute to inadequate communication between education and work institutions. Exclusionary hiring practices and policies resulting from the labor surpluses of a deep recession may remain even as recovery commences since large institutions are seldom immediately responsive to change.

This chapter speaks to problems that arise out of all categories except a significant aspect of the first—job shortages caused by a deep recession. There is no way that the youth employment condition can be discussed without recognizing that we are only slowly recovering from a depression and that we still have total unemployment rates as high as they were in the worst of the recession in 1958, and that was the worst post-World War II period prior to 1974–75.

We cannot treat parts of the body separately, however, when there is a systemic infection. We cannot talk of expanding youth employment opportunity if it is to be done at the expense of adult employment. It is difficult to focus the attention of employing institutions on rigid personnel practices that exclude youth when they simply do not need more employees of any age. This brings us to another predicament in the United States. Growth, as traditionally measured, is falling far short of producing the number of jobs needed. It is further strained by shortages of irreplaceable materials and by inflation. At the same time there is an unrelenting demand for access to opportunities heretofore denied minorities, women, and, increasingly, those retired into nothing by a technological economy. How we deal with the total situation will affect youth employment.

This chapter has more modest dimensions, but some aspects of the quantity of opportunity can be dealt with on a selective basis without charting a whole new future for maturing industrial economies. It is, of course, more productive to focus on our unsolved problems than to extol our successes. But it should not pass unnoticed that we have accommodated a growing population of teenagers to a surprising degree. Teenage employment has risen by 93 percent over the last twenty years, compared to an increase of 30 percent for the population as a whole. Black teenagers did not, however, get their share of this remarkable employment growth. And, although the teenage labor force increased more rapidly than the regular one, unemployment among teenagers did rise, particularly in 1975, as the full impact of recession was felt.

Most of the growth in teenage employment involved part-time jobs. It is becoming increasingly commonplace for teenagers to be going to school *and* working. In fact, the teenage labor force is on its way to becoming a student labor force, raising a question as to whether their inclusion in the total figures confuses or illuminates either the youth situation or the total situation. Other nations do not even include students in their statistics on the labor force and unemployment. There is little question that the dynamics of the student labor market greatly swell the figures reflecting teenage unemployment.

These general observations are necessary background before examining a series of eight specific aspects of the youth employment condition that are set forth here as a basis for further discussion. No attempt was made to impose order on the categories listed, for most problem areas are an amalgam of several or all of the categories.

There is a major division of the youth labor market into "youth-type" jobs and "regular" jobs. No precise distinction can be made between "youth-type" and "regular" jobs, and not all jobs youth hold fall clearly into one category or the other. It is, nevertheless, necessary to recognize the distinction. At the same time that we have enlarged opportunities for students to work part-time and for younger out-of-school youth to hold jobs in the service sector, there seem to be increasingly rigid barriers to the entry of youth into the jobs supplied by larger firms, that is, jobs of the kind held by adults where the connection between employer and employee is less tenuous and there are opportunities for advancement.

The phenomenon of holding youth out of the "regular" job market is identified in several studies of employers' hiring practices conducted over the last half dozen years. A national study put out by the Bureau of Labor Statistics,[1] a two-city study by Daniel Diamond and Hrach Bedrosian,[2] a study of forty corporations by the National Manpower Institute,[3] and a study in a rural area of the South[4] establish that from two-thirds to four-fifths of employers do not hire for regular jobs until the ages of twenty or twenty-one.

A major longitudinal study beginning with tenth graders in 1966 shows that two years after graduation high school graduates do no better than dropouts in finding employment. This is to be expected if ages twenty or twenty-one are the magic ages to get regular jobs.[5] The ramifications of this gap between the age society certifies youth as having completed public schooling and the age most employers hire for regular jobs are many and beyond full exploration here. But this fact is related to many of the points to be made in the remainder of this chapter.

The kind of local information that would make the youth labor market function more smoothly is inadequate. While we have a growing body of data on the national youth labor market, it is the local labor market where most youth must make their mark in the employment world. Yet, as Seymour Wolfbein recently commented, most data in this field lacks "sufficient geographical detail."[6] In a recent comprehensive study of work measurements, Willard Wirtz and Harold Goldstein acknowledge that the reporting of the Bureau of Labor Statistics "is recognized nationally and throughout the world as a model of accuracy and efficiency," but they go on to provide an extensive analysis from a local standpoint and to offer detailed recommendations for improvements.

The Occupational Outlook Handbook represents a pioneering effort, again from a national perspective. It is, however, more of a reference tool for counselors than an aid for students. There was an effort to collect information on current job vacancies in the late 1960s, but it was abandoned. There is no way of knowing where the jobs are now in a local labor market, let alone where they are going to be in the next five or ten years. And we have scarcely begun to inventory training opportunities available to youth in the community or to establish the kind of links between those who seek training and those who offer training opportunities, links of a kind that now exist between job seekers and job offerers through public and private employment agencies.

There have been attempts to use computers to transmit occupational information directly to students. There are about a half dozen computer systems of differing complexity in use in an expanding number of areas, but they vary as to the kind of local information fed into them. All suffer from the lack of any systematic attention to the provision of local data. The Department of Labor now has about ten state-wide projects underway as part of its new National Occupational Information Service.

Placement services for students entering the labor force are practically nonexistent. The step beyond providing information is placement in an appropriate job. What is needed is a means of aggressively seeking job openings from employers and matching them to student applicants. Activity of the United States Employment Service with regard to students in their senior year has steadily declined, although there has been some effort recently to reverse this trend. What is needed is joint effort among schools, the U.S. Employment Service, employers, and unions, but there are only a few beginnings along this line.

Markets, however, also require brokers, and the school labor market does not have one. A placement service seems the most likely mechanism to link school and work, but most schools do not have placement services, although there are now some excellent models to build on. The responsibilities would extend far beyond finding jobs for students leaving school. Schools would learn something about local employment, local employers, and unions. Counselors would have an opportunity to observe employment conditions. Information provided by those placed in jobs would then be helpful in determining the curriculum. Employers would have a means of relaying to schools what they thought the educational deficiencies were among the youth placed with them.

There is a shortage of counseling resources, particularly for youth not planning to enter college directly upon high school graduation. According to the best estimates available, there is only about one person-year of counseling time available for each thousand students in the high schools, and most of that time goes either to help those who plan to attend college with their selection or to perform miscellaneous duties frequently assigned school counselors by harried school principals.

But the availability of counseling is not the only problem. The orientation of counselors, which is perhaps changing now, has been away from the local employment situation, even though that is the one faced by four out of five students entering the full-time labor force without a college degree. Instead, efforts are bent toward encouraging and arranging continued schooling and attempting to find a professional counseling method in the jumble of psychiatric and clinical psychology treatment models. The need is not just for more counselors, but for counselors who are better trained in their professional schools, who are aware of the character of the world of work, who are willing to work with those who choose to begin working rather than to go to college, and who keep up with the local employment situation.

The problem also extends beyond merely providing more professional counselors with a different orientation. There is the whole community from which to draw in preparing youth to make employment decisions. Counselors should be able to design and manage programs utilizing the larger efforts of employment assistance specialists, paraprofessionals, teachers of classroom teachers, rosters of employed citizens willing to spend time with young people, and the rich and often ignored resources of business establishments and union headquarters. There has been a breaking down of traditional job titles in the educational system, and it has produced new efforts to draw more effectively on community resources under the rubric of "career education." The result has been a broadening of the concept of teaching itself. So it is the function that is important, and there is no attempt here to define professional jurisdictions.

In employment counseling it is hard to specify exactly what professional expertise is, or if, indeed, what is involved is even a profession in the commonly understood sense of that word. It still remains that, beyond the many resources useful in making decisions about what kind of employment to seek or to prepare for, there is a need for people to make it their business to know as much as they can about employment or at least to know where to find those who do know.

The transition from school to regular work is usually abrupt; the transition needs to be eased for many more young people. As underdeveloped as the practice is, we seem to have had more discussion of the idea of phased retirement than of phased entry into the labor force. There have been "work experience," programs, and a small percentage of students have been exposed to "cooperative education" programs in high school. Only about 10 percent of the graduating class of 1972 ever participated in such programs, however. Most of what now exists would fall short of constituting any truly cooperative relationship between a community's employers and unions and its school system in an effort to move youth gradually out of education and into employment. And if one were to add the additional dimension of doing it at a rate adjusted to the kind of work involved and the individual youth's own rate of progress in completing his education and learning a skill, it might be hard to find even a single example.

Many students are, to be sure, employed, and it affords benefits that are not being undervalued here. It takes place largely as an arrangement arrived at solely between student and employer, however, and neither expects the work to be full-time when the student leaves school. As desirable as this may be, it has little relation to the idea of phased entry into the labor force just mentioned. There is no particular logic to a practice of keeping youth entirely in an educational bureaucracy for twelve or more years, letting them scramble for temporary "youth jobs" for four more years or so while they wait to meet the age requirement for commencing regular jobs. This separates life into time traps—youth for education only, adulthood for just work, and old age for nothing. Here is where we could start to break out of the pattern.

The advantages of such phasing are advanced here entirely for the purpose of dealing with problems related to the youth labor market. The objective is to rationalize the entry mechanisms that merge youth into the employment lane. There is, of course, the related but different and important dimension of combining classroom learning and experience in ways that will improve the educational and developmental process. This broader consideration cannot be developed here, but the increasing acceptance of experience as a means of education fits well with the idea of gradual experience as a means of smoothing entry into the labor market.

The merging of education and experience is not easy. Also, in the doing of it there are matters that must be carefully considered. It cannot, as was said earlier, be done at the expense of jobs for adults. Nor can it become a new source of cheap labor that can be used to undermine wages. The surest guarantee on these matters is to consult unions concerning the design and supervision of work experience programs.

Perennial questions about keeping skills training in the public schools relevant to the demand for skills are usually answered in the wrong terms. Keeping the skills taught in the public schools attuned to the needs of the labor market through occupational projections is difficult. The considerations involved in selecting specific job skills in vocational education are broader than the making of projections.

First, there is need to abandon the debate over whether, as a matter of educational principle, any job-specific skill training should take place in the school classroom at the secondary level. If approached as a matter of principle, such a debate applies equally to the majority of postsecondary studies, including law and medicine. The question is more pragmatic: What is the best way to acquire the skill needed for the desired job and at the same time get the most one can by way of a general education?

A second need is to recognize that projections showing growth in a particular occupation or industry do not make that occupation or industry a safe area in which to teach job-specific skills. What is needed is the expansion of knowledge to include hiring and training practices in those occupations and industries. Do they hire before the age of twenty-one? If not, what does a seventeen-year-old vocational school graduate do with the skills he has learned in that growing occupation? Does the industry prefer to do its own training? If so, could there perhaps be a cooperative relationship between the school and employers in that industry? Does the industry expect to get trained students directly from school and actually hire them when they have completed school? If so, would it be appropriate to equip youth with skills that would enable them to get those jobs? Answers to these questions require an understanding of the behavior of local industry—and contact between schools and industry if there is to be understanding.

Yet a third need is to integrate public and private skill training through the development of cooperative relationships between public schools and good proprietary schools that would expand a student's training options without requiring the student to drop out of public school. Why cannot public school students be placed in courses in good private schools, and tuition be paid from public education funds if such an arrangement would provide access to a desired occupation?

Aside from the effects of recession, there are just not enough opportunities for students to gain experience or enough productive roles for out-of-school youth. While the deep recession is the largest reason for inadequate experience and employment opportunities, there is another adverse trend. It is a long-term decline in youth employment opportunity in the inner city. Regular employment rates, for a variety of reasons, do not tell the full story. A better measure is simply the proportion of all teenage youth who are employed. In 1954 the proportion of white teenagers employed was 43 percent, compared to 38 percent of black teenagers—a significant difference, but certainly not a dramatic one. By 1974, however, the proportion of white teenagers employed had risen to 49 percent, while the proportion of black teenagers employed fell to 26 percent, and, by 1975, the proportion of black teenagers employed had dropped even further—to 23 percent.

The service sector jobs to which teenagers are admitted are fleeing the inner city. Retail trade, car washes, and fast-food chains are expanding, instead, on the suburban rim. Perhaps all this has been said so often we have become immune, but it also means that teenage youth are being eliminated from the labor market in the central cities. This shortage of opportunity in the central city is easy to identify, but it becomes even more widespread if young people have no chance to combine classroom study with quality experience. That shortage may have to be balanced by community service, that is, work that everyone knows needs to be done, even when the economy is not producing enough regular jobs.

Work is not keeping up with the changing world of education. The education-work relationship is most frequently discussed in terms of whether education is adapting fast enough to keep up with "the changing world of work." A proper consideration of the operation of the youth labor market ought to give some attention to whether there are adjustments needed on the work side as well.

As for education, we now move all of our youth through elementary school and three out of four through high school. Half of those who finish high school go on to college. There have been many innovations in the structure, attitudes, and practices of postsecondary education, and enrollments at community colleges continue to grow despite "steady-state" forecasts based on population trends. The offerings in postsecondary education become even more diverse, in both content and style, which affords a wide latitude of career choices in the student period of life. The freedom to choose a worthwhile career and the further liberating effect of a good education on the mind are increasingly being bestowed on the nation's youth.

There is, however, at least strong circumstantial evidence that industry is not demanding higher educational requirements as rapidly as the working population is achieving education. The brief for this possibility would contain some of the following points:

—There has been a major observed shift toward a service economy over the last quarter of a century. On closer inspection, this appears to reflect heavily the fact that the rising proportion of women in the labor force is concentrated in the service sector. The occupational distributions of men and women (looked at separately) are not that much changed.[8]

—A study combining the work of two researchers (reported in *The Job Content of the U.S. Economy, 1940-1970)* concluded that the average "general educational development" required to perform the jobs in the economy advanced from 10.0 years in 1940 to only 10.5 years in 1970, and that the years of training time to learn the jobs rose from 1.8 years to 1.9 years in the same period of time.[9]

—Each decade, many college graduates take jobs held earlier by people without college educations. A study of this phenomenon concluded that, if we did the jobs of today at the educational levels of the people who actually performed those jobs in 1940, we would require 55 percent fewer college graduates than are now employed.

There are, to be sure, many jobs that require ever-longer educations, particularly in professional and technical occupations. But when we point to higher growth rates in some of these occupations, we forget that actual numbers are relatively small. A recent dissertation established that, of the 385 occupations identified by the Bureau of the Census, 70 of the occupations could account for nearly 70 percent of all jobs; just 35 could, therefore, account for half of the jobs.[10] A look at the list of occupations and the numbers of jobs in them provides some understanding of the slow growth of average educational requirements. The first professional group to make the list (elementary and secondary teachers) is in fourth place. The next professional group (registered nurses) is in eighteenth place, preceded, among others, by truck drivers, janitors, and sewers and stitchers.

If Freud were rewriting *Civilization and Its Discontent* today, he might have something to say about the possibilities of discontent in a civilization where the abilities of its people are getting far beyond what can be, or is being, done with them. The only thing clear about the situation described here is that we are talking about an education-work disjuncture that is occurring on the side of work. This could suggest that we should retard our educational growth to match the pace of the work place, but this would be wrong. There is no possible conception of an overeducated society without a rejection of most of the values on which our society has been established.

There is interest in what can be done to make jobs more rewarding from the standpoint of content as well as pay. This interest is not parochial; it is international. It is evidenced in a publication of the International Labor Organization entitled *Making Work More Human* and in a report of the Organization for Economic Cooperation and Development, which, in 1975, admonished member countries that: "Individual development and human satisfaction must become a responsibility of the world of work as well as the world of education." Although it has not gotten very far, the effort to make jobs more rewarding should not be abandoned just because the task is difficult. A prime mover in this effort, James O'Toole, writes: "To really improve the quality of working life requires hard work, careful planning and diagnosis, commitment, time, and a willingness to abandon old ideas. . . ."[11]

From global considerations, go back to the high school class of 1972 in the United States. When asked their occupational aspirations, 54 percent wanted to be professional and technical workers, although just 14 percent of the labor force was holding such jobs in 1972 and was expected to be holding them in 1985. By 1974, the reality of the situation affected those aspirations, but just slightly. Half of the class still aspired to professional and technical jobs. Are we headed toward a showdown when those young people find that the jobs are not there? Will their predecessors, who went to the colleges in the 1960s and made their views known on campus and to the world, accept what they find in the world of work when they have had time to try it on for size? We just do not know. But bringing work into closer relation to education is offered here as being a valid goal.

The amount of space devoted to each of these points is not meant to denote their relative importance. Rather, it indicates that some have received more attention of late than others. In each case, some aspect of "what to do" has been suggested to trigger further thought and discussion. What has likely been observed as the thread running throughout is the extent to which work institutions and educational institutions are isolated, one from another, and the absence of even practical links between school and work.

While all of these matters have their programmatic aspects, it is, in the end, a new process that is most likely to fit the pieces of the puzzle together again. What is needed is *collaboration* among those elements of community that have control over some segment of a youth's life and opportunity, and it must occur in the community—where the schools are, where the jobs are, and where the youth are. The National Manpower Institute has suggested pilot efforts to increase such collaborative ventures (Community Education-Work Councils), and, in conjunction with the Department of Labor, is creating a consortium of twenty such communities that have substantial efforts under way. This example is used only to illustrate the basic point: that *participation* of education, labor, industry, voluntary agencies, parents, students, and effective citizens will be required to create a smoothly operating "youth labor market." The fruits of these efforts must be weighed in the future, but the importance of trying to provide connections among the key institutions has been demonstrated.

NOTES

1. Thomas Gavett *et al., Youth Unemployment and the Minimum Wage,* Bulletin 1615 of the U.S. Bureau of Labor Statistics (Washington, D.C.: Bureau of Labor Statistics, 1970), 75.
2. Daniel Diamond and Hrach Bedrosian, *Industry Hiring Requirements and Employment of Disadvantaged Groups* (New York: School of Commerce, New York University, 1970).
3. National Manpower Institute, *A Study of Corporate Youth Policies and Practices* (Washington, D.C.: National Manpower Institute, 1973).
4. Charles Rogers *et al., Teenage Unemployment in Two Selected Rural Counties in the South* (Raleigh, N.C.: Center for Occupational Education, North Carolina State University, 1969).
5. Jerald Bachman *et al., Youth in Transition,* Volume 3 (Ann Arbor, Mich.: Survey Research Center, University of Michigan, 1971).
6. Seymour L. Wolfbein, "Informational and Counselor Needs in the Transition Process," in *From School to Work* (Washington, D.C.: National Commission for Manpower Policy, 1976), 175.
7. Willard Wirtz and Harold Goldstein, *A Critical Look at the Measuring of Work* (Washington, D.C.: National Manpower Institute, 1975), 1.
8. See Willard Wirtz, *The Boundless Resource: A Prospectus for an Education-Work Policy* (Washington, D.C.: New Republic Book Co., 1975), 88, for a detailed comparison.

9. James G. Scoville, *The Job Content of the U.S. Economy* (New York: McGraw-Hill Book Co., 1969).

10. William C. Deyo, "A Census-based Occupational Clustering System for Career Education," unpub. diss., Cornell University, 1976.

11. *Work and the Quality of Life,* ed. James O'Toole (Cambridge, Mass.: M.I.T. Press, 1974), 15.

10. Conserving Human Resources: The School Dropout

Ralph W. Tyler

The employment of youth has suffered as a result of increasing isolation from the adult working world. I want to emphasize that there are also serious, adverse effects of this isolation on the development of youth and on their opportunity to make a smooth transition into constructive adult life. As background for understanding the problem, it is useful to examine the demand for education created by a democratic industrial society, the underlying expectations of young people as they grow into adulthood, and the part that school and out-of-school experience plays in the education of young people.

There are three major functions of education in our society. One is to enable young people to acquire the understanding, skills, and attitudes required for constructive participation in the economic, political, and social life of a democracy. Another is to allow for mobility within the society. One of the strengths of a democratic society is its openness, which enables positions of responsibility and leadership to be filled by people with talent, energy, and ambition, regardless of social class. In the last generation about one-half of the adults in America advanced up at least one rung in the social ladder, and only one-quarter moved down. The last of the functions is to help each person achieve all that he is capable of achieving.

As our society continues to utilize science and technology, and as the nation continues to raise its expectations, the educational requirements for most people to participate constructively, to remain socially mobile, and to fulfill themselves are higher. Most school dropouts, who have no plans for further formal education, may not be adequately prepared to participate fully in a democratic society, to advance to a higher social level, or to achieve their full potential.

It must be recognized that the experiences through which a person learns the things required for living today include much more than the school experience. Experiences in the home, social activities in the community, chores and jobs, participation in religious activities, reading, listening to the radio, watching television—all are included in the actual educational system through which one acquires knowledge and ideas, skills and habits, attitudes and interests, and basic values. In the past, experiences in the home, at work, with religious institutions, and at school had the strongest influence on the development of youth in this country. These were the experiences that helped young people acquire basic habits—orderliness, punctuality, and attention to work—and their sense of values.

Attitudes toward productivity and basic working skills were learned as young people performed chores at home or held part-time jobs (mowing lawns, shoveling snow, preparing meals, doing the laundry, carrying newspapers, working in stores or shops) where they worked under close supervision and were subject to critical appraisal. Learning to take responsibility for a task and accepting the consequences of success and failure in performing it are important aspects of education for adult roles that are not primarily learned in school. Adolescents commonly vacillate between the desire to take responsibility and fear of failure. Hence, learning to take responsibility and to bear the consequences require experiences that allow a gradual increase in the degree of responsibility and in the seriousness of the consequences of failure, paralleling the increase in competence and confidence that is also part of youth. The school alone contributes little in the way of learning experiences for this kind of growth.

The school does contribute to the development of social skills that are essential to civic life, to home living, and to effective work in service occupations, that contribute to group settings in all vocations. Schools are societies in microcosm, where children and youth communicate, cooperate, and compete. Generally schools operate without serious conflict and without rousing intense antagonism, and they appear to contribute positively to the development of social skills essential in many adult situations.

In educational systems of the past, the essential parts had certain interdependent features. A student's interest in learning what the school sought to teach was usually stimulated in other parts of the system—the home, the working place, the social life of the community. The school did not need to motivate the majority of the students to learn. Skills (reading, writing, and arithmetic) developed in the school were useful activities outside the school, particularly activities related to work and recreation. Skills that are not often used, however, soon become inoperative. Hence, any total educational system needs to provide an opportunity to practice what is initially learned.

The educational system is, therefore, more than the school system. In the recent period of rapid social change, educational roles of the home, the community, religious institutions, and places of employment have changed greatly, and the influence of all but the school appears to be less. The school is maintaining approximately the same role with the same amount of time spent annually in working with children and young people. Time lost in other kinds of experiences is taken up in different ways, including watching television and peer group activities. Schramm and Parker report, for example, that the average American child between the ages of ten and fourteen spends about 1,500 hours per year viewing television and only about 1,100 hours per year in school.

With the great erosion of out-of-school educational opportunities, particularly for young people living in remote areas and in inner cities, especially minorities, there are more people for whom the educational requirements—that they become constructive participants in a democratic society, that they apply their talents and energies in a way that allows them to achieve social mobility, and that they reach their full potential—are not being met. This represents a loss of human assets in that society.

Most young people look forward to becoming adults. They recognize that this means being independent and taking on more serious responsibilities. As they feel themselves becoming physically mature, they need reassurance that they can become adults in other respects as well. The increasing isolation of youth provides little opportunity for young people to test themselves in an adult world in association with other adults. They see themselves as barred from adult work, adult participation in social and civic affairs, adult responsibilities, and adult satisfactions. Some respond with protests or destructive acts. Some become alienated and withdraw from the larger society. Many lose the self-confidence required to initiate action and to work independently. Socially constructive attitudes develop in a society that seems to care for youth and to reward those who care for others. Social habits and skills require conditions in which they can be practiced. The knowledge about society that adults seek to teach falls on dead ears if it is contradictory to direct experience.

At present a considerable fraction of American youth are not developing into mature adults, proud of their unique characteristics, and participating constructively and effectively in the maintenance and development of the society in which they find themselves. Many are not finding self-realization. This, combined with the lack of a smooth transition into adult work channels, poses problems for even the successful student; it is a major tragedy for the young person who drops out of school.

In Chapter 9, Paul Barton has emphasized what should be a basic recommendation: *Bring work into closer relation to education.* I would expand this to include a new and better-planned coordination of education with all of the important sectors of the community that have potential for furnishing significant learning experiences for youth: industry; agriculture; service agencies, both public and private; religious institutions; youth organizations. There are many such influences. I would also recommend the establishment under public auspices of a community education council responsible for identifying the inadequacy of opportunities for the full development of youth and the encouragement of institutions, organizations, and other groups to fill the gaps.

Because many communities are either small or lack sufficiently varied work and service opportunities to provide within their borders all of the opportunities that should be available, I would recommend the establishment in each metropolitan region of a regional council. Such a council would work with the community councils to provide opportunities on a regional basis that communities cannot provide within their own borders.

State legislation may be necessary to establish these councils under public auspices and to support them. The intent of these recommendations is not to establish a second public education system; it is, rather, to give public sanction and support to reconstructing the total educational system that has been eroding. It depends largely upon the renewed and redirected efforts of existing institutions and the continued encouragement of volunteer efforts.

PART THREE
School Programs for Youth in Transition to Adulthood

11. Educational Programs for Youth in Transition: Implications of Kohlberg's Research for the Schools

Edwin Fenton

During the past twenty years, Lawrence Kohlberg, his colleagues, and their graduate students have been carving out new fields of psychological and educational research. They have also made substantial contributions to moral philosophy and to the philosophy of education. Three words, "cognitive moral development," capture the essence of their work. "Cognitive" stresses organized thought processes. "Moral" involves decision making in situations where universal values, such as the sanctity of life and the need for authority, come into conflict. And "development" indicates that patterns of thinking about moral issues improve qualitatively over time.

Kohlberg's research has significant implications for the transition from adolescence to adulthood. Kohlberg equates mature moral thought with what he calls the principled stages. Few people attain these principled stages of thought before their twenties, and they can reach them readily during their twenties only if they have developed the preconditions for stage advance while in adolescence. Given these preconditions, they are prepared for the move to principled moral thought that can accompany appropriate collegiate experiences.

This paper has been adapted with permission from an earlier draft prepared by the author for the Institute for Developmental Educational Activities, Inc., the educational affiliate of the Charles F. Kettering Foundation. The author gratefully acknowledges support from the Danforth Foundation, which made possible the research on which this chapter is based.

Schools and colleges can play vital roles in facilitating the transition to adulthood in the moral realm. But educational programs must be carefully designed if they are to help students reach this goal. To indicate the nature of the role of the schools in moral education, this paper summarizes some of Kohlberg's research, examines the role of educational institutions in moral development, and describes programs of educational intervention based on cognitive developmental principles.

RESEARCH FINDINGS

People think about moral issues in six qualitatively different stages arranged in three levels of two stages each. Table 11-1 delineates these levels and stages.

The most reliable way to determine a stage of moral thought is through a moral interview. A trained interviewer presents a subject with three dilemmas, each of which sets forth a situation for which the culture lends some conventional support for a number of actions which the protagonists could take. A dilemma from one of the interview forms follows.

> Joe is a fourteen-year-old boy who wanted to go to camp very much. His father promised him he could go if he saved enough money for it himself. So Joe worked hard at his paper route and saved the $40 it cost to go to camp and a little more besides. Just before camp was going to start, however, his father changed his mind. Some of his friends decided to go on a special fishing trip, and Joe's father was short of the money it would cost. So he told Joe to give him the money he had saved from the paper route. Joe did not want to give up going to camp, so he thought of refusing to give his father the money.

After presenting the dilemma, the interviewer asks the following questions:

1. Should Joe refuse to give his father the money? Why?
2. Is there any way in which the father has a right to tell the son to give him the money? Why?
3. What is the most important thing a good father should recognize in relation to his son? Why that?
4. What is the most important thing a good son should recognize in relation to his father? Why that?

5. Why should a promise be kept?
6. What makes a person feel bad if a promise is broken?
7. Why is it important to keep a promise to someone you don't know well or are not close to?

Over a period of twenty years, Kohlberg and his colleagues have identified typical responses to the questions on the moral interview at each of the six stages of moral thought. Scorers compare the responses given by the subject to these typical responses in order to determine moral stage. Trained scorers show 90 percent agreement in identifying stage despite the difficult and sophisticated scoring techniques involved in scoring qualitative, open-ended data.

A stage is an organized system of thought. Presented with several moral dilemmas, a person who reasons predominantly at Stage 3 will consistently give Stage 3 answers, although the content of the dilemmas may vary widely. For example, Stage 3 thinkers will argue that they should do what pleases or helps others whether the issue involves obeying the law, affection between friends, or reasons to punish people.

Three responses at one stage to a single moral problem may illuminate the nature of a psychological stage. Suppose that Jill steals a sweater from a store. The store's security officer accosts her companion, Sharon, who is Jill's best friend. He tells Sharon that she will get in trouble unless she reveals her friend's name. Here are three responses to this dilemma, all at Stage 2:

> Sharon ought to tell. After all, Jill walked out and left Sharon to take the rap. Sharon should give as good as she got; that is fair. Why should she get in trouble for Jill when Jill walked out on her?
>
> Sharon should not tell. The store probably charges enough to cover a few rip-offs. All the stores do that. It is just for Jill to get back something that she and all the rest of us have paid for anyway.
>
> Sharon should not tell. Neither the storeowner nor the security guard ever did anything for her. So it would not be right for her to help them out by giving Jill's name.

These three responses differ in the act they recommend (which Kohlberg calls the content of thought) since two say that Sharon should not give Jill's name and the third says that she should. They also define what is fair or just or right in different terms. But the underlying structure of thought is the same. Each response invokes an element of fairness based on reciprocity, on mutual back scratching.

Table 11-1

Levels and Stages of Moral Development

Level	Stage	Orientation	Description
PRECONVENTIONAL: People consider the power of authority figures or the physical or hedonistic consequences of actions, such as punishment, reward, or exchange of favors.	1	Punishment and obedience	Physical consequences of doing something determine whether it is good or bad without regard for its human meaning or value. People think about avoiding punishment or earning rewards, and they defer to authority figures with power over them.
	2	Instrumental relativist	Right reasoning leads to action that satisfies one's own needs and sometimes meets the needs of others. Thought often involves elements of fairness, but always for pragmatic reasons rather than from a sense of justice or loyalty. Reciprocity, a key element, is a matter of "you scratch my back, and I'll scratch yours."
CONVENTIONAL: People value maintaining the expectations of their family, group, or nation for their own sake and regardless of immediate consequences. People show loyalty to the social order and actively maintain, support, and justify it.	3	Interpersonal sharing	Good behavior is equated with whatever pleases or helps others and with what others approve of. People often conform to stereotypical ideas of how the majority of people in their group behave. They often judge behavior by intentions and earn approval by being "nice."
	4	Social maintenance	This orientation is toward authority, fixed rules, and the maintenance of the social order. Right behavior consists of doing one's duty, showing respect for authority, or maintaining the given social order for its own sake.

PRINCIPLED: People reason according to moral principles that have validity apart from the authority of groups to which they belong.	5	Social contact, human rights, and welfare orientation	Right action is defined in terms of general individual rights and standards that have been examined critically and agreed upon by the society in a document such as the Declaration of Independence. People stress the legal point of view, but they emphasize the possibility of changing laws after rational consideration of the welfare of society. Free agreement and contract bind people together where no laws apply.
	6	Universal ethical principle	Right is defined as the decision of conscience guided by ethical principles such as respect for human personality, liberty compatible with the equal liberty of all others, justice, and equality. These principles appeal to logical comprehensiveness, universality, and consistency. Instead of being concrete rules, they are abstract ethical principles.

Table 11-2

Levels and Stages of Perspective Taking

Level	Stage	Description
PRECONVENTIONAL: People have the perspective of an isolated individual rather than that of a person who belongs to a group or social system.	1	The person focuses only on his or her own interests and does not think of himself or herself as a person with responsibilities to others or as a person who belongs to a group.
	2	The person still wants to serve his or her own interests, but is able to anticipate another person's reactions. Here there is willingness to make a deal to get what one wants.
CONVENTIONAL: People assume the perspective of a person who is a member of a group or of a society.	3	The person sees things from the viewpoint of shared relationships, such as caring, trust, respect between or among individuals who know each other.
	4	The person can take the viewpoint of a member of a social system or of society as a whole. The person is able to see a situation through the eyes of many actors, including people in the society whom he or she does not know.

This common element in the thought is its structure, its underlying organizational pattern.

An individual reasons predominantly at one stage of thought and uses contiguous stages as a secondary thinking pattern. For example, a young teenager might respond to moral dilemmas in Stage 3 terms 70 percent of the time and employ Stage 2 thought the remaining 30 percent. This person is finishing the transition from Stage 2 thought to Stage 3 thought. Another person who responds at Stage 3 approximately 70 percent of the time and at Stage 4 approximately 30 percent probably stands at the beginning of the transition to Stage 4 thought.

These stages are natural steps in ethical development, not something artificial or invented. To find them, Kohlberg gave moral interviews to people of different ages and then classified responses on the basis of the similarity of the reasoning process that was used. Subsequently he conducted a longitudinal study, interviewing the same fifty subjects every three years. The longitudinal data helped him to revise and clarify his statements of the stages.

Kohlberg's initial research was conducted in the United States. Parallel cross-sectional research, however, has been conducted in a number of additional countries including Turkey, Mexico, Taiwan, Israel, Yucatan, Canada, and India. In each of these countries, researchers have found the same stages of moral thought that Kohlberg discovered in the United States except that the principled stages (Stages 5 and 6) do not appear among respondents interviewed in traditional societies.

People can understand moral arguments at their own stage, at all stages beneath their own, and sometimes at one (and occasionally two) stages above their own. They generally prefer the highest stage of thought that they can comprehend. James Rest interviewed forty-seven high school seniors using the standard Kohlberg moral interview. He was able to determine the stage of moral thought that they could generate spontaneously in this way. Then he gave them a set of prepared statements giving responses to a moral dilemma at all six stages of the Kohlberg scale. He asked them to recapitulate the statements in their own words and to rank the statements in terms of how convincing they were.

Rest drew four conclusions about the comprehension of moral stages from this experiment. First, subjects tended to get nearly all of the statements at any one stage right or to get nearly all of them wrong. Second, subjects who got nearly all statements at a given stage right also successfully recapitulated the statements at all stages lower than their own. Third, comprehension scores declined rapidly for stages higher than the subject's own. Although most Stage 3 subjects comprehended Stage 4, they did not comprehend Stage 5; only 40 percent of Stage 4 thinkers comprehended Stage 5 arguments. Fourth, the highest stage used on the responses to the moral interview was a better predictor of comprehension than the predominant stage which a subject used.

There were two major findings about preference. First, 80 percent of the subjects preferred the highest stage of thought that they comprehended. Second, subjects tended to prefer the higher-stage statements in their developmental order—that is, they preferred a Stage 5 argument to a Stage 4 one.

People move through these stages in invariant sequence, although any individual may cease developing at any stage. Children begin to reason at Stage 1. Most children then move to Stage 2 during the primary or elementary school years. As early as nine but usually several years later, most Americans then move to Stage 3 thought, and some pass into Stage 4 during middle or late adolescence. The transition to Stage 5 takes place, if at all, when people are in their late teens or their twenties, or even later in life. This transition usually accompanies collegiate experiences. Very few people attain Stage 6 thought, and those who do are often older than thirty. In short, the development of moral thought is a slow process that can continue throughout one's lifetime.

The development of moral thought can also be arrested at any stage. Perhaps 20 percent of adult Americans continue to reason at Stages 1 or 2; about 30 percent use Stage 3 thought, and another 40 percent employ thought at Stage 4 most of the time. Less than 10 percent reason predominantly at Stage 5, and a tiny proportion (1 percent), at Stage 6. In summary, most stage movements which typical Americans undergo—from Stage 2 to Stage 4—take place during adolescence, and those who move to Stage 5 do so mainly in the five or ten years after adolescence ends.

Two major factors limit the development of higher stages of moral thought. The first is limited cognitive capacity, that is, a limited ability to use formal, abstract thought. Beginning formal operational thought on the Piagetian scale is a necessary but not a sufficient condition for Stage 3 moral thought, and more complete formal operational thought is a similar prerequisite for Stages 4 and 5 thought on the Kohlberg scale. Many people who think at the early formal operational level still reason at Stages 1 or 2 morally, while most people who are fully formal operational do not reason at Kohlberg's Stage 5.

The second factor which limits the development of higher stages of moral thought is a limited social perspective or role-taking ability. Kohlberg's colleague, Robert Selman, defines role taking in two ways: by the way that an individual differentiates his or her perspective from that of other individuals, and by the way in which an individual relates these perspectives to each other. As is true for attainment of a given cognitive stage, attainment of a given stage of social perspective is a necessary but not a sufficient condition for reaching a stage of moral thought. The important levels and stages in developing perspectives are described in Table 11-2. They parallel levels and stages on the moral scale.

Higher stages are better than lower stages. Psychological evidence supports this claim. As we have seen, people develop through the stages in invariant sequence. If lower stages were better cognitively than higher ones, we would be forced to argue that the quality of thought deteriorates as a person matures, a proposition difficult to maintain. But the psychological argument that higher stages are cognitively better than lower ones rests on a firmer basis. Higher stages of thought are cognitively more differentiated, more integrated, and more universal than lower stages. More differentiated means that, at higher stages, people distinguish between such different things as the value of life and the value of property. At Stage 1, people do not make this distinction. More integrated means that, at higher stages, people place such values as life, law, and property in a hierarchy. Life logically ranks higher than property because property sustains life, not the reverse. More universal means that higher stages appeal to more universal principles, such as the social contract, equality, or justice. Lower stages stress less encompassing principles, such as avoiding punishment for oneself or gaining a personal reward. Hence, higher-stage thought is cognitively better because it is more consistent than thought at lower stages. Higher-stage thought also solves problems that cannot be solved at lower stages.

Stage transition takes place primarily because encountering real life or hypothetical moral dilemmas sets up cognitive conflict in a person's mind and makes the person uncomfortable. Take Mary, who customarily reasons at Stage 2. Mary thinks in terms of reciprocity—

I'll help her because I want her to help me next time. Then she hears the argument that people will like you more if you help them. They will approve of you because good people help each other, and that is a good thing to do for its own sake. This higher-level reasoning makes Mary uncomfortable because it challenges her customary belief, and it appeals to her because people prefer the highest stage of moral thought that they can comprehend. She sees the difference between the two arguments and prefers the one at a higher stage. As this paragraph implies, stage change at the two lower levels (Stages 1-4) is mainly cognitive and symbolic and does not require large amounts of personal experience.

Kohlberg believes, however, that two different sorts of "personal" as opposed to vicarious-symbolic experience facilitate the transition to principled thought. The first involves leaving home and entering a collegiate community where students encounter conflicing values in the context of moratorium, identity questioning, and the need for commitment. In such an environment many students move to Stage 5 thought, particularly if, as a part of their collegiate experience, they receive explicit cognitive-moral stimulation through moral discussion programs organized, for example, as part of a course in moral philosophy. The second sort of "personal" experience arises when people face crises of the sort so many faced during the Vietnamese War. Both soldiers who served in Vietnam and students who resisted the draft confronted conflicts between law and conscience, between Stage 4 morality on the one hand and principled thought on the other. This traumatic conflict produced a transition from Stage 4 to Stage 5 thought in a number of the subjects studied by Kohlberg's group.

Deliberate attempts to facilitate stage change in schools through educational programs have been successful. Within the last decade, more than a score of investigators have attempted to facilitate stage change by leading moral discussions. They have worked in elementary schools, in junior and senior high schools, and on the college level. Although results vary in detail, one generalization about this research stands out: compared to the students in control groups, students in experimental groups who participated in moral discussions showed significant increases in the stage of moral thought they commonly used.

In these programs, Kohlberg and his colleagues used hypothetical moral dilemmas to trigger moral discussions, particularly in social studies and English classes. The dilemmas presented situations for which the culture lent some conventional support for a number of actions that the protagonists could take. Teachers presented dilemmas in a variety of forms: oral, written, recorded, taped, filmed, videotaped, or acted out in skits or role-playing exercises. The discussion leader then attempted to get students to confront arguments one stage above their own. Such a confrontation takes place either when students who think at contiguous moral stages discuss reasoning or when the teacher poses a higher-level argument through a probing question or a comment.

IMPLICATIONS FOR CIVIC EDUCATION

The transition from adolescence to adulthood in the United States implies that one takes on new responsibilities as a full citizen in a democratic society. The schools should prepare students for those responsibilities, and yet there is a virtual consensus that conventional social studies programs have failed to achieve this vital goal. The research of Kohlberg and his colleagues suggests both reasons why conventional programs have failed and guidelines for programs more likely to succeed.

A comprehensive program of civic education should have five sets of goals: (*a*) to acquire knowledge about the political system and the way it works, (*b*) to develop intellectual skills essential for solving civic problems, (*c*) to develop other skills required for full participation in a democratic society, (*d*) to develop a value system compatible with the principles that underlie democratic institutions, and (*e*) to develop self-esteem so that an individual will feel worthy and able to participate in civic life.

Knowledge

The research of the Kohlberg group has three vital contributions to make to the teaching of political knowledge. This research specifies the level of cognitive development required to understand the Constitution either as a societal maintenance document (Stage 4) or a social contract document (Stage 5). It also indicates the levels of social perspective (Stage 4) required before a person can understand how a political system embracing fifty states and more than 215 million people works. Finally, it demonstrates how stage development will lead to a more sophisticated understanding of basic concepts, such as justice or authority, that are involved in civic education.

The principles underlying the Declaration of Independence and the Constitution are Stage 5 principles. The Constitution can be viewed as a social contract designed to guarantee the rights of citizens. These rights, Kohlberg argues, are not merely the ones on which Americans agree; they are universal rights—justice, liberty commensurate with the equal liberty of all others, and equality—that should be valued in all complex societies. One glory of the Constitution is that a small band of gentlemen farmers and business people recognized the universality of these principles. They wove them into a document that set up a government designed to protect basic rights. The founders must have known that people who did not understand or agree with the principles they espoused would sometimes hold the reins of government. They built into the Constitution certain devices intended to protect fundamental rights when they were threatened. One dramatic demonstration of the effectiveness of these protective devices was the resignation of President Nixon under pressure from the Congress and the courts. The wisdom of the members of the Constitutional Convention was once again confirmed.

Most students who graduate from American high schools do not understand the Constitution as a Stage 5 document. Although we have no national sample, experience with large numbers of high school juniors and seniors suggests that most have not attained full Stage 4 moral thought and that almost none think predominantly at Stage 5. Many people can comprehend one stage of moral thought above their own and prefer the highest stage of moral thought they comprehend. As a major goal of civic education, every student should develop the ability to understand the Constitution and be able to subscribe to it with informed consent. In order to achieve informed consent students must attain at least Stage 4 thought on the Kohlberg scale. This will not happen without a comprehensive program of civic education extending throughout the school experience and designed specially to raise the stage of moral thought.

The Constitution can also be viewed as a Stage 4 societal maintenance document. The government it sets up and the laws passed by that government attempt to prevent the outbreak of domestic discord, protect the nation from its enemies, and promote the general welfare. In order for this government to succeed, citizens must be willing to take part in governmental activities and to obey the laws that legislators pass. The research by Rest indicates that many but not all Stage 3 thinkers can understand this position. As an irreducible, minimal goal of civic education, we should strive to bring this understanding within the grasp of high school graduates.

Many programs in civic education teach the Constitution over and over again—in fifth grade, eighth grade, ninth grade, eleventh grade, and twelfth grade, but it bores many students. Who would not be bored by reading a document that lacks meaning? Rather than "teaching" the Constitution repeatedly, those who teach civics should help them develop the formal operational thought, the full societal perspective, and the higher stages of moral thought required to grasp the meaning of basic governmental documents. Then they could study the documents meaningfully in senior high school.

Now to the matter of understanding how the political system works. Many teachers assume that students have a sophisticated understanding of such terms as "the society" or "the nation." Most students do not. They have limited social perspectives and limited role-taking abilities. They think of themselves as isolated individuals or as members of small groups of people with whom they are personally acquainted. I have been struck repeatedly with the limited social perspective of typical high school students engaged in moral discussions. Students argue that a person should lie to protect a friend who has been shoplifting because one owes something to a friend but not to the shopkeeper, who is a stranger. They find themselves unable to take the shopkeeper's place in this situation or to empathize with his problems. They also are unable to realize how society would be affected if everyone condoned stealing and no one helped to enforce laws. What does the term "society" mean to such students?

A person cannot understand how the political system works without a full societal perspective. At its best, our political system tries to promote the welfare of all citizens—farmers, laborers, storekeepers, students, and older Americans. These people's lives and their well-being are inextricably interrelated. Students who lack a societal perspective lack the cognitive capacity to understand interrelatedness. Many of the generalizations in civics and history texts are beyond their comprehension. A societal perspective is a necessary but, again, not a sufficient condition for understanding how the political system works.

Most programs in civic education assume that this understanding exists or that it will develop without special learning experiences during a yearlong course in government or civics. Any proposal for a new senior high school course in the political process implicitly assumes that students will reach eleventh or twelfth grade with the capacities needed to understand the materials they will use. Most of them will not. A fully effective civic education program must cultivate students' cognitive abilities, perspective formation, and moral development through a number of years if most students are to reach twelfth grade with the societal perspective they need to understand how the political system works.

Kohlberg's research also bears on the ability of students to deal with concepts fundamental to the political system. People define concepts in stage-related terms. For example, here are five definitions of the word "fair" at five stages of the Kohlberg scale:

1. Fair means that you got rewarded for doing something good by an important person.
2. Fair means that if you helped me out, I should help you out.
3. Something is fair when all of us in the group agree that it was the right thing to do.
4. Fair means that something was done according to the rules, even if the rules may have seemed wrong.
5. Fair means that people got the rights that they were guaranteed in the Constitution.

When a teacher uses the word "fair" in class, students may take the word to mean any of the five definitions given here. Many vital civic education terms—such as law, authority, justice, rights, and equal treatment—will be defined by students in stage-related terms. Is it possible to study civic affairs intelligently with any definition of these terms under a Stage 4 (societal maintenance) level. If the answer is "no," then we must begin to facilitate stage development at an early age and press the matter with every resource at our command.

Intellectual Skills

By intellectual skills I mean primarily problem-solving abilities, often called analytical inquiry skills by the New Social Studies projects of the 1960s. The effort to teach these inquiry processes in the classroom failed with all but relatively able students. They did not succeed with less able students for three major reasons. First, they require full formal operational thought, that is, the ability to hypothesize, to see all possibilities in a situation, to relate evidence to inference, and so forth. Only about half of American adults reason at full formal operational levels according to a study by the Kohlberg group. Second, they require a full societal perspective when they are applied to most civic problems: Should we have forced busing? Should we close factories which do not abide by pollution regulations? Third, they require a sophisticated understanding of social science concepts, which, as we have seen, many students lack.

Although the New Social Studies represents a significant advance in civic education, curriculum projects have not provided a satisfactory solution to the problems involved. Traditional civic education taught students facts and generalizations about American society and its history and attempted to instill in them a love of country and its institutions. The social studies projects shifted the focus of civic education toward the intellectual processes required to solve civic problems. But the projects failed to provide the antecedent conditions that would enable students to use these sophisticated intellectual processes. Civic educators must now find ways to facilitate the development of formal operational thought, societal perspective, and higher-stage moral thought if they expect to educate students who can use the inquiry processes stressed during the 1960s. The work of Kohlberg and his colleagues provides guidelines for this difficult, demanding, and important task.

Participatory Skills

Good citizens require participatory skills that can be classified into two levels. The first level consists of data-gathering and communication skills essential for playing an active part in any civic organization. The second level uses these basic skills for negotiation, working out compromises, or influencing political decisionmakers. Both these levels of skills must be carefully taught.

The community meetings that are the heart of the civic education schools being organized by the Kohlberg group in Cambridge, Massachusetts, and Pittsburgh, Pennsylvania, provide a setting in which these skills can be learned and practiced. To participate effectively in a community meeting, students must have the following skills: reading, listening, speaking, reporting, chairing a meeting, doing committee work, working constructively in small groups, and controlling disruptive persons. Taking part in community meetings demonstrates the need for all of these skills and provides instructors with an opportunity to teach them. Students learn skills far more rapidly and thoroughly when they learn them for a purpose than they do when these skills are taught divorced from an immediate need to use them. Most students, however, require carefully planned educational experiences before they can master basic communication skills.

Community meetings also provide a forum in which students can practice higher-level participatory skills. In community meetings, staff and students together develop rules to govern themselves; they also implement the rules they make. In both processes they must develop the ability to compromise when differences of opinion arise and learn to negotiate if they wish to persuade others to support their point of view. They must also learn how to influence key people in the decisionmaking process. These second-level skills should transfer to the wider political system outside the school. To assure transfer, they should be buttressed with formal study of such issues as how to influence decisionmakers in the city council or a labor union and with practice in vital processes such as this.

Participatory skills and the development of higher stages of perspective formation and moral thought go hand in hand. Students use participatory skills to make decisions in community meetings. For example, they may have to decide what to do about a member of the school who has broken the rule against using drugs. As they use participatory skills to gather information and to communicate their ideas, students put themselves in the role of protagonists in the case. They listen to people with a more fully developed societal perspective who argue that the whole community may fall apart if it cannot enforce its own rules. And they hear arguments at several stages of the Kohlberg scale. Processing real-life moral dilemmas in community meetings should develop participatory skills as well as lead to perspective formation and advances in the moral stages that enable students to attain the intellectual goals of civic education discussed earlier.

Developing Democratic Values

I have already touched upon this topic at many points. The arguments can be summarized under the following eight points:

1. There are Stage 6 universal values—respect for persons, justice, liberty compatible with the equal freedom of others, and the equality of persons—that underlie democratic society.
2. The Constitution represents an attempt through a social contract to assure citizens of these basic rights.
3. Every student capable of formal operational thought should be educated enough to understand the principles underlying our government in order to be able to subscribe to the Constitution with informed consent.
4. To understand the principles which underlie the Constitution, a

person must attain at least Stage 4 (social maintenance) thought in the Kohlberg scale.

5. The development of higher stages of moral thought can be facilitated through the discussion of hypothetical moral dilemmas in formal classes and through processing real-life moral dilemmas in participatory governmental structures.
6. Moral dilemmas should be built around a series of universal values identified by Kohlberg: punishment, property, affection, authority, law, life, liberty, and distributive justice.
7. These value issues lie at the heart of the problems central to good instruction in the social studies and to the great works of literature used in the English curriculum.
8. In order to develop an adequate program for civic education, a school must foster developmental goals over a number of years and make cognitive development, perspective formation, and moral development the central goals in the curriculum. Lawrence Kohlberg and Elliot Turiel ("Moral Development and Moral Education," in *Psychology and Educational Practice,* ed. George Lesser [Chicago: Scott, Foresman and Co., 1971], 414) state the case for a developmental approach to moral education in the following terms:

> *It is constitutional.* Simulation of universal stages of moral reasoning is not indoctrination. It violates no civil rights and is independent of any religious doctrines or assumptions.
>
> *It is philosophically justified.* Moral philosophers throughout history have in various ways expressed or elaborated principled moral judgment; almost all moral philosophers, as well as moral leaders like Abraham Lincoln or Martin Luther King, have [had] an ethic based upon an advanced stage of moral development. The moral stages do not represent an American middle-class-value bias; they are universal.
>
> *It is socially useful.* Persons at a higher level of moral development not only reason better, but they act in accordance with their judgments. Experiments demonstrate that principled persons act more honestly and live up to their beliefs in the face of inconvenience and authority more than do people or children at lower stages.

Developing Self-Esteem

Kohlberg's research does not speak directly to the problem of developing self-esteem among students. The nature of higher moral stages, however, implies the importance of this curriculum goal since respect for persons and the equality of persons are two of the major attributes of principled thought. Clearly a democratic polity requires citizens with a high level of self-esteem. They should feel able to participate actively in the political life of the nation. They should know that they have the skills needed to make their influence felt. They should feel that what they think is important and that other people would benefit from listening to their opinions. How can civic educators foster such attitudes?

Preliminary anecdotal evidence indicates that participation in the community meetings conducted by the Kohlberg group in Cambridge has fostered self-esteem. Many students reported in interviews that they believed that other students in the school respected their opinions. The chance to participate in community decisionmaking where academic excellence was a requirement for success evidently increased self-esteem, particularly among students who had limited academic potential. Being able to join teachers in decisionmaking also had its impact. In community meetings it is clear that each vote counts for something since all decisions are made by majority rule and since the size of the electorate (about seventy students in Cambridge) is small. Everyone can contribute something to such a group, and everyone can recognize the contribution that he or she can make. The fact that students know that they have a considerable degree of control over their environment seems to have contributed positively to their self-esteem.

Properly led, moral discussions can also enhance self-esteem. In a moral discussion, students and the teacher should sit in a circle in order to encourage the exchange of opinions and to facilitate sensitive attendance. The teacher should consistently acknowledge the contributions of students by attempting to clarify what they say and by making a student's comment the focus of discussion. Everyone, even students who cannot read or those who never do homework, can contribute constructively to a moral discussion. The stimulus material, a dilemma in written or audiovisual form, can be introduced in class. Everyone can have an opinion about a dilemma because everyone has an opinion at some moral stage about every moral problem. A skillful teacher can encourage nonvolunteers to participate by telling them before class that they might be asked from time to time to paraphrase a comment by another student or to identify a point of difference between two students who disagree with each other. Many students testify that they have taken a more active role in a moral discussion than they have in any other classroom activity, and that they enjoyed it. Like community meetings, moral discussions can be used to work toward several sets of objectives simultaneously. All of these objectives will contribute to a well-rounded program of civic education in American schools.

Kohlberg's research suggests that comprehensive civic education programs must have six interrelated elements. First, they must extend over many years of schooling. Stage change develops slowly. Typical students who have participated in programs of moral discussions as part of a year's social studies course have risen in moral reasoning by a third to a half stage compared to students in control groups. No one single course, no matter how carefully constructed or taught, will do the job. No one has as yet measured the effects of programs covering several consecutive years of intervention. But there is every reason to believe that stage change will accelerate year after year.

Second, a comprehensive program of civic education must extend well beyond the social studies. Every discipline in the school can help to facilitate the development of formal operational thought which is a prerequisite to Stage 4 (social maintenance) moral thought. Every teacher, as many athletic coaches well know, can help to improve the self-esteem of students. The entire instructional staff can make lower-level participatory skills an explicit curriculum goal. In addition to social studies teachers, English instructors can give moral development and the formation of social perspectives a central place in their course goals. Civic education is far too vital and sophisticated a matter to be left exclusively in the realm of a twelfth-grade government course.

Third, a comprehensive program of civic education must change the hidden curriculum as well as the overt curriculum made up of formal classwork. The hidden curriculum involves all the institutional arrangements from which students learn in school. These arrangements include the ways in which school rules are made and enforced; the ways in which teachers and administrators use their power and their ability to praise or sanction; and the ways in which the sheer size of large, impersonal schools affects students' learning. In many schools the hidden curriculum denies what formal courses in civic education affirm. Student governments lack the power that civics textbooks claim belongs to elected bodies in a democracy. School rules are made autocratically instead of through the democratic process studied in government class. Schools fail to provide the checks and balances and the mechanisms for appealing decisions of authorities that students read about in the Constitution. Under these conditions, the fundamental changes in school governance that have taken place in the experimental democratic unit in Cambridge become more important.

Fourth, a comprehensive program of civic education must include an intensive, long-run teacher preparation program. Traditional teachers will have much to learn—and much more to unlearn. They must learn to think in terms of new sets of educational objectives. They must learn how to facilitate the development of social perspective and moral stage by leading moral discussions and participating in community meetings. They must learn to relinquish some of their power to a community in which each person, faculty member and student alike, has one vote. And they must learn to use and to develop new curricular materials. These instructional, administrative, and curricular skills grow slowly, and they must be learned through experience. We cannot prepare teachers for their new roles in civic education by giving them a book to read or by organizing workshops on occasional in-service days.

Fifth, a comprehensive program of civic education requires new curricular materials organized for developmental goals in both social studies and English. These new materials should provide sequential and cumulative learning experiences throughout the student's high school career. They do not exist, even as prototypes, at the present moment. But a psychological, philosophical, and educational rationale for such materials does exist, and there are individual curriculum artifacts that were developed in the curriculum projects of the 1960s that can be adapted to developmental goals. Finally, there are a substantial number of experienced curriculum developers who can turn their attention to this task once they internalize the research findings and the intervention techniques summarized at the beginning of this chapter.

Finally, a comprehensive program of civic education must be evaluated carefully to determine progress in reaching all five sets of goals—political knowledge, intellectual skills, participatory skills, values, and self-esteem. Evaluators already have the tools for this task in their test instruments and techniques of participant observation. A truly comprehensive evaluation should follow at least one sample of students far beyond the end of their high school careers. A civic education program can be proclaimed successful only if the students who participate in it become more effective citizens than those who do not. Perhaps the time has come for another Eight-Year Study, this one directed to one of the primary goals of education in a modern democracy: the preparation of young people to contribute constructively to the democratic processes that have sheltered and weaned them and given them opportunity to grow as free and responsible human beings.

12. Action Learning in Minneapolis: A Case Study

Diane Hedin and *Byron Schneider*

More than the omnipresent bell, more than the Carnegie unit and the state's custodial mandate, it is the restrictive climate of the school that imposes rigid accountability for time and artificial measures of achievement and confines youth. Its very atmosphere inhibits both the natural and rational transition of youth to constructive adulthood. As an institution, it resists change and tends to blur more fundamental issues.

Just a short time ago an action-learning coordinator commented:

> The problem is that, instead of spending our time arranging challenging learning situations for Lynda Mattson, we spend *all* of our time trying to convince her teachers that she might benefit from an hour-long experience each day *outside* of this building. Making sure she is back to her next class on time seems to be a much more important issue to some members of this faculty than whether she is learning more inside or outside this school building.

The public is concerned about the fundamental issues that are the goals of education. It is concerned about methodologies, content, and youth. The public questions how to best educate young Americans. Many teachers and young people are angry, frustrated, or bored, and no amount of reshuffling the curriculum will satisfy them. The goals of education have become amorphous, and they are not shared. In many districts there is lack of purpose. It has been charged that schools are "saturated with inertia and in their present form are almost unmovable."[1] Even that charge is not so devastating as the conclusion by Project TALENT that "high school education as a whole serves no useful purpose."

Pupils realize that educational values are confused and inconsistent. They know that, except for a few teachers and administrators, the schools would be paralyzed, and that it is those few who provide creative educative experiences for youth, both in school and in the neighborhoods. They are the energizers. It is those few in Minneapolis, Minnesota, who popularized the notion of action learning and stimulated planning throughout Minnesota and the Twin Cities area. This chapter is a brief case study of the first two years in the development of action-learning programs in seven junior and senior high schools in Minneapolis, with special emphasis on the two pilot schools, Southwest Secondary School and Central High School. The two pilot schools serve contiguous, yet very different, attendance areas and populations.

Central High School is an inner-city school that, during the past five years, has attracted an intellectual and socially mixed student body through a magnet program for high achievers. Its students, in grades nine through twelve, come from diverse middle- to lower-class socioeconomic backgrounds, and much of the student body is black. The integrated faculty is young, relatively inexperienced, and willing to experiment. The median age for teachers is thirty-two years old, and most have taught for fewer than five years.

In sharp contrast, Southwest Secondary School is located in a remote corner of the city and sheltered from the rest of the city by lakes that are bordered by wealthy suburban communities. The school has an almost entirely white, upper-middle-class student body oriented toward further education. The faculty, which serves pupils in grades seven through twelve, is tenured, conservative, traditional, and cautious. The median age of the faculty is forty-six years old, and the average number of years the members have been teaching is over twenty.

The other five schools, which became a part of Project ACT in the second year of the project (1976-77) are Bryant and Anthony Junior High Schools, South and West High Schools, and Marshall University Secondary School. All serve students from diverse racial and socioeconomic backgrounds.

PROJECT *ACT*

The proposal accepted and funded by the Danforth Foundation envisioned urban pupils "*A*ffirming Our *C*ity *T*ogether" (Project ACT). The program was intended to enrich the secondary curriculum by offering action-learning opportunities in *all* subject matter areas and at *all* grade levels in *all* Minneapolis secondary schools and to develop a model for voluntary racial and socioeconomic integration by providing opportunities for students of various backgrounds to learn and serve together in off-campus settings.

The three-year pilot program was viewed as an initial step toward redesigning the secondary curriculum of a major city's public school system in an attempt to increase student involvement in the life of the community. The ultimate goal was to provide opportunities for all secondary students in Minneapolis to participate and interact with persons of different ages and backgrounds, and with different lifestyles; to explore larger sections of economic, political, and social life; to engage in responsible work and volunteer activities; to have more active and practical learning; and to make worthwhile contributions to their communities.

In Project ACT, action learning is defined as learning through a combination of direct experience in the life of the community and association instruction or reflection. Some activities that may be considered to be action learning are volunteer service, internships, social and political action, community surveys and studies, shadowing a person to explore a career, and living in another culture. It is the characteristics of the experience, not the student's actual job or task, that seem to be more important determinants of the educational value of the activity. Such activity would give young people the opportunity to perform tasks that both the student and the community think are worthwhile; to have some responsibility to make important decisions within their project or placement; to work on tasks that challenge and strengthen thinking, both cognitive and ethical; to have others depend upon their actions; to work with peers and with adults in group efforts to achieve common goals; and to systematically reflect on out-of-school experience.

THE THEORETICAL FRAMEWORK

This chapter is not meant to be theoretical; rather, it presents a description of the organization, staffing, scheduling, crediting, and evaluation of Project ACT. It seems appropriate, however, to summarize the theoretical arguments both as an introduction to the chapter and as the basis for a more detailed description of the program.

The Social Development of Youth

The most compelling reason for offering action learning to young people in the Minneapolis schools relates to their social development and has been well documented by six national commissions and panels that have studied adolescent development and secondary education in the past several years.[2] While the several panels differ in style and substance, they agree on one major finding: the barriers between youth and the larger society can be reduced by increasing student participation in the "real" world outside the school. All the reports note with concern that adolescence, because of extended schooling, has become a stage of life best characterized as a "holding period," an interval during which youth are expected to bide their time, to observe but not participate in adult life, and, most of all, to enjoy themselves and keep out of trouble.

Those who work with young people intuitively know that there is something wrong with our socialization process when adolescence, the stage of life when energy and sometimes idealism are highest, has become a time when waiting is the central task. There is little opportunity, either in school or elsewhere, for a young person to be a contributor or to be recognized as one, to experience the satisfaction of undertaking a needed task and completing it creditably, to feel the joy and endure the pain of significant participation in the world, or to act instead of always preparing for action. Youthful privatism, apathy, cynicism, hostility, and even delinquency are some of the consequences of treating young people as if they were incompetent, childish, and superfluous.

Although most of the attention has been focused on the immediate effects of separating youth from adults and from serious and responsible participation in the adult world, there are also long-run costs that society must pay for inadequately preparing youth for adulthood, including a reduced capacity for youth to accept the responsibility for themselves and for the fate of others and a weakened concern for the welfare of the total community. For educators and school administrators to ignore this problem or even to respond with nothing more than colorful and up-to-date curricular materials and classroom methods is to misread the seriousness of the situation and to neglect a responsibility. Schools are where youth are, and it is inescapable that schools must encourage youth to participate in the broader life of the community.

The benefits of action learning can also be weighed in such terms as better communication, less vandalism, and more adequately prepared adults, but even this is still to miss a critical point in the argument for these programs. The same television documentary that laments "wasted youth" may include a litany of pressing social problems without ever noting an obvious link. Youth is not just a resource to be developed for the future; it is available now to be used in the fight for a better society. Perhaps the schools in Project ACT can be converted from isolated centers of learning to participating community institutions. Perhaps they can be centers to which students not only come to learn but from which they go out into the community to use what they have learned, to add their strength, talents, and energy to those who are tackling society's problems.

If action-learning programs do nothing more than fulfill the young person's need to be, and be recognized as, a contributing member of society, that would justify their place in the schools. Yet we dare hope for even more, that the skills and habits learned in community involvement programs will carry over into their adult years. Longitudinal data that support or refute the claim that such programs will help develop adults who can function effectively as parents, workers, and citizens are not yet available. We can at least hypothesize that this approach is as likely to have these consequences as more traditional fare conveyed through lectures, movies, readings, and discussions.

The Psychological Development of Adolescents

A further rationale for Project ACT is derived from theories of developmental psychology grounded in the educational philosophy of John Dewey and spelled out by Jean Piaget and Lawrence Kohlberg. The key concepts, only superficially summarized here, are that human beings move through distinct stages of moral (social) and cognitive growth. Each stage is a unique way of interpreting experience and understanding the world. Whether or not growth and development occur from stage to stage depends on the quality of the interaction with the environment. The crucial point is that growth does not automatically occur. Instead, a person needs significant interaction with the environment to promote movement to higher stages of development.

The developmentalist would not argue that learning through direct experience alone is sufficient to achieve developmental growth. While experience is often a good teacher, it is not necessarily a good teacher, as history so painfully demonstrates. We have all met a person who tells us pompously that his judgment is superior because he has been in the "business" for twenty-five years. But does he mean twenty-five years or one year times twenty-five? From a developmental standpoint, learning includes two basic spheres of activity: *significant experience* interacting with *careful reflection.* Merely providing students with lectures, readings, or exhortations accomplishes little.

The practical implications of developmental psychology for Project ACT, it would appear, are that there is a need to provide students with new, stimulating, and challenging experiences, with the opportunity for significant social role taking (the process of taking the perspective of another), and time for careful reflection. Failure to do this may result in the cessation of a person's psychological—both personal and intellectual—growth.

Academic Development

Action-learning experiences directly contribute to students' academic growth, as well as their intellectual growth. An experience-based learning model that requires students to pursue or apply acquired knowledge and skills through direct involvement in nonclassroom settings makes traditional classroom approaches even more effective.

First, the opportunity to do something significant with what is taught in the classroom has the potential of increasing the student's motivation, as he begins to see the connection between what he learns in school and experiences in the world and feels the tension created by his own personal investment in the outcome. We have had, for example, students sit with rapt attention while we read the state regulations concerning standards for nursing homes. They listened because they were angry about the way the elderly were being treated in the facility where they had volunteered to help. Their motivation came from personal contact with the problem, a demonstrated need for information, and a serious intent to apply what they learned. In action-learning programs, students have opportunities to generalize and transfer their learning to problems existing outside the school. Critical thinking skills, including moral deliberation, become more than an academic exercise to fill class time when a student must decide whether to question the treatment of children in an institution for the retarded. One of our students, for example, was shocked to learn that children who misbehaved were put in a dark closet, euphemistically known as the "quiet room." She had to weigh the consequences of challenging this policy. Was it important enough to speak out against what she considered inhumane treatment of people to risk being considered "troublesome" and possibly lose her volunteer position?

Action-learning programs give students the opportunity to gather original data about a social or political issue and to "reality-test" both their own conclusions and those presented in the classroom or a text. A student interning in the city attorney's office was able to observe how race and social class can influence the pattern of sentencing, and then compare this reality against the concept of equal rights for all Americans presented in the textbook.

Service learning provides an arena in which both to practice what is learned and to evaluate the usefulness of acquired knowledge and skills. Allowing students to do a survey for a community organization helps them see the advantages and pitfalls in using this method. They and their teachers might even wonder whether knowing this technique will be of the slightest use to them in their adult life.

Through applying school learning, the student also receives feedback that allows him to see his success or to recognize his errors and receive help in correcting them. Once again, active participation engages the student in the application of what he knows, believes, and can do. When a student acts on his concern for the environment, uses his knowledge of chemistry to check for pollution in a stream, applies his knowledge of the political-legal system to finding ways to halt pollution, or combines his knowledge of facts with his ability to communicate them to others, he is engaged in the acid test of all learning: Can it be applied effectively in making a positive difference in the world?

Educators are as reluctant as anyone else to apply what they teach or preach. Consider a basic principle learned in an introductory course in economics; the law of diminishing returns. When applied to the classroom, it indicates that successive applications of similar material by similar methods in similar settings, perhaps by similar people, will have progressively less impact on students and may even reach a point of negative return.

The contrast between the wide-eyed enthusiasm of first-graders and the glazed-eyed boredom of twelfth-graders is painful and compelling evidence of the decreasing influence of classroom experience. By the time a person is a senior in high school, he has already sat through more than twelve thousand rather similar hours of classroom instruction. Many have been inoculated so often that they have become immune to the method and weary of the setting.

Despite daily reminders that teachers are faced with the impossible task of entertaining hostile audiences for thirteen years of their lives, they somehow cling to their faith in classroom instruction. They would do well to consider Arthur Schlesinger's gentle admonition:

> We alone know how limited and marginal our impact generally is on the boys and girls, the young men and young women, delivered by their families to our passing and inevitably superficial care. We do the best we can, but we do not have it within our power to repair all the inadequacies of the family, the church, the marketplace, the media, and other social institutions, although they have it within their power to blame us for not doing so.[3]

Perhaps a qualitatively different method, such as action learning, is more likely to engage and motivate students than another dose of classroom instruction. Action learning is no panacea, but it does offer a completely new kind of experience. Because of the novelty and the accompanying challenge, such experiences are often found to be satisfying and enjoyable. This is not a trivial outcome. We are all inclined to repeat satisfying experiences. And if the experience of high school can be satisfying, we will have made an important step toward helping young people make an effective transition to adulthood.

There is not much intellectual excitement in discussing mundane matters such as scheduling, staffing, crediting, and organizing a school program after the more interesting descriptions of student action, service, and research. Programs stand or fall, however, on how well the staff solves the organizational problems of integrating new experiences into the existing school structure. The organizational considerations that follow will, we hope, assist secondary school personnel attempting to work action learning into a rigid and inhospitable school structure.

IMPLEMENTATION

Staffing

There were several patterns for staff utilization. At three of the schools, Southwest and Marshall University Secondary Schools and

Central High School, an action-learning office was established and staffed by half-time coordinators who assisted those faculty members using youth participation in their courses. In three other schools, Anthony and Bryant Junior High Schools and South High School, the teachers involved in Project ACT had no coordinator and worked primarily with students enrolled in action-learning courses and programs they themselves taught. In only one school, West High School, did the teacher function as both coordinator and teacher of action-learning courses.

Coordinator Model

The coordinators in the schools that used this model were faculty members who continued to teach half-time but served as action- learning coordinators for the balance of the day. This staffing pattern allows coordinators to stay in touch with the reality of the classroom and to identify with their fellow teachers, which is important in winning acceptance for a different program.

The coordinator's major task is to encourage other faculty members to develop action-learning options in their subject matter areas by offering ideas and suggesting activities that supplement and enrich existing course offerings. A suggestion made over lunch seems to produce better results than announcements at faculty meetings, and the coordinators know which faculty members would be receptive to various community options. Informing teachers about program potential has been undertaken in several ways. There is a graduate course, offered through the University of Minnesota and taught by the project director that is available to faculty. The more effective way of informing teachers, however, has proved to be informal individual contact between teachers and project staff.

Coordinators also make contact and arrange for community experience, for this is a time-consuming process that would put a heavy burden on classroom teachers. At times they help supervise students after they are placed (if their regular teachers are unable to do so), or they substitute for teachers who wish to make their own contacts, supervise students, or work along with students in community projects. Besides helping action-learning teachers find long-term community placements or internships, coordinators encourage their colleagues to use field trips, to invite resource people to the classrooms, and to arrange short-term projects that promote more intensive action-learning activities. The major thrust of the coordinator's job is to work with other teachers, but they also supervise and advise the small number of students in service-learning projects that cannot be incorporated into existing courses.

The Teacher Model

In this model the staff members involved in Project ACT planned and taught their own action-learning course or program. At Bryant and Anthony Junior High Schools, action learning took the form of a three-hour interdisciplinary program offered by a team of three teachers in each building. Approximately ninety students each semester enrolled in this alternative program in each school. The students were placed in internships or volunteer assignments and conducted research in the wider community in addition to more traditional classroom work in three subject areas. (At Bryant, the action-learning program combined English, social studies, and science; at Anthony, it combined social studies, art, and science.) At South High School, a social studies teacher offered thirty students a different two-hour action-learning course each trimester involving psychology, political science, and sociology. The rationale for these courses was that, in order to have a significant impact on the students' citizenship development, a blending of direct experience in the forms of field trips, resource people in the classroom, internships, and community research must be combined with substantial classroom experience.

This model has advantages over the coordinator model. First, the teachers with the most interest, experience, and enthusiasm for action learning have direct contact with the students. Learning experiences can be more effective and powerful than is possible with the coordinator model, where the ACT staff input is limited to advising and assisting other faculty members who offer the experience-based course. Second, the role of teacher is more comfortable than that of coordinator, for coordinators also have administrative and catalytic functions. Because a coordinator is available to the total faculty, however, many more students and teachers can be involved in the program. A substantial portion of the faculty in a school must accept and participate in action learning if it is to make the school a resource for the community rather than an isolated tower of learning.

Relationship to the School Structure

Finding significant ways to involve young people in the social, political, and economic arena did not prove nearly as difficult as incorporating those experiences into the curriculum. That is why examples of student action appear in the context of their place in the curriculum. The following typology represents the way in which students presently participate in our community. It represents a continuum from the least integration into the school curriculum, on the left, to the greatest integration, on the right.

Least integration ——————————————→ Greatest integration

I	II	III	IV	V
Uncredited activities	Independent study in the community	Enrichment for existing courses	Action-learning courses and programs	Sequence of courses and experiences

Uncredited Activities

During the two years that Project ACT has been operating, approximately four hundred students have participated in community activities arranged by the action-learning offices just for the experience. The students have received no academic credit. In some cases work was done during a student's unscheduled time or during a study period and in some cases students were released from classes to allow them to serve in the community. The option was used as little as possible because the faculty members objected to such assignments. Only when a mutually agreeable arrangement between students, coordinator, and teachers (and at times parents) is achieved can a student miss regular classes. For example, several Southwest Junior High School students were released for the last two hours of one school day each week to assist in an after-school program for retarded youngsters. They teach youngsters to swim, to play basketball, to get along with "normal" children. They learn patience, responsibility, and sensitivity. Their teachers agree that little irreversible harm results from their absence from class for a few hours a week.

At Marshall University Secondary School, eight seniors spent one afternoon every week at the General Mills Research Laboratory for a full academic year. The students received no credit and were required to make up the work they missed in school. And yet, the experience of working along with scientists and laboratory technicians conducting experiments in food science research was considered so valuable that more than seventy more students later applied for the program. Both laboratory staff and school staff agreed that it was a superb learning experience, and it is to be increased to a full day per week, with students receiving academic credit for participation.

After-school activities, such as participation in career exploration through the Explorers Program or Junior Achievement, are also facilitated by action-learning coordinators. Cooperating with these and other youth organizations allows the staff to offer many more options than they otherwise could. Through Explorers, students learn about the food industry by working in a research laboratory at the Pillsbury Company; they shadow hospital staff to learn about the medical profession, they work in pet clinics and at the Humane Society to explore veterinary medicine as a vocation. In another uncredited after-school program, twelve students were trained to become "researchers" in facilities for delinquent youth through a project sponsored by the University of Minnesota. After receiving training in participant observation and ethnographic research methods, they lived for several days in group homes and treatment facilities to learn about therapeutic programs. Without the assistance of the action-learning staff, it would have been very difficult for these students to be released from several days of school to conduct their "research."

In spite of the quality of such volunteer service and internships, uncredited learning activities have two major shortcomings. First, only a small segment of the student population seeks out such experiences. Many who volunteer are already more competent and resourceful than their classmates. Most students are anxious to amass as many credits as possible and shun noncredit activities. The separation of the community experience from the classroom experience also often deprives the student of the chance to maximize his learning. Experience may be the best teacher, but the ability to draw accurate and useful lessons from daily events must be deliberately developed and nurtured. The classroom experience has the potential for helping students maximize their learning from field experiences.

Independent Study in the Community

The major difference between independent study and uncredited activity is the awarding of credit following successful completion of independent study in the community. An essential difference, as far as the continuum is concerned, is that off-campus community activity with limited supervision is performed outside the context of a regular school course.

In Minneapolis, students may receive elective "action-learning credit" in all subject matter areas. Approximately 150 students enrolled each year have this option. Students outline what they wish to do, for how long, for what purposes, and perhaps what outcome. This outline is reviewed by a faculty member and a program coordinator. If approved, the student acts on the proposal. A senior with a strong interest in creative dramatics, for example, wanted to direct fifth-graders in a play. Since there was no existing course through which she could do this, she signed up for the Action-Learning option in English. Her progress was reviewed and monitored by a speech and drama teacher; her day-to-day work was supervised by an elementary teacher.

Special learning opportunities organized, staffed, and administered outside the student's home school, programs like "Executive Internships" and "Close-up," fall into this same category. The school releases students for a certain period of time and may grant credit for the experience. Fifteen students are involved in a program called "Teenage Health Consultants," sponsored by a consortium of health clinics. Students receive action-learning credit in health for attending eighteen training sessions on mental health, juvenile rights, drug use, birth control, human sexuality, and nutrition, and for preparing and presenting information on these topics to high school and junior high school classes. They lead discussions in group homes and youth agencies, run information and referral centers in their schools, make video tapes on such topics as sexual assaults, and relate to other students on a one-to-one basis. In order for a student to receive credit for this experience, a health teacher reviews work completed under the supervision of agency staff.

Programs such as this offer exceptional opportunities to students, but they may not have much impact on the teaching style and curriculum of the school. Unless faculty members have more than nominal involvement, valuable insights are lost. Such models do establish the precedent of viewing community members, who are not certified teachers, as competent to facilitate accredited learning experiences.

Enrichment for Existing Courses

Project ACT has made it possible to introduce a community action component into several subject areas with little or no immediate change in curriculum, school structure, or staff deployment. Students in existing courses use either short- or long-term community action as a way to "reality-test" course content, gather data and examples, and make use of what is learned in the class.

In two years more than 1,100 students have participated in the community through the enrichment option. In the following examples, a variety of short-term and long-term research, service, observation, and social action enlivened instruction and learning in areas at Central and Southwest Secondary Schools.

—Students in woodworking classes spend two class periods each week supervising and teaching a woodshop for first and second graders in nearby elementary schools. They team-teach with retired persons. Other students in the class visited and spoke with skilled cabinetmakers and furniture repairmen at large department stores and small neighborhood shops to find out what jobs were available with skills learned in the course.

—Then there were approximately seventy-five students in a sociology class who had a firsthand view of possible career choices and community problems by spending approximately twelve to twenty hours in a community placement office. Other students learned about anesthesiology in a hospital, about auto mechanics in a body shop, about printing in a neighborhood printing shop, about the problems of the elderly in a nursing home, about the legal system in a county attorney's office, about being an accountant in a large corporation, about police work by attending the police training academy, and about becoming a veterinarian from a doctor at the "Kitty Klinic."

—Students in a psychology class are "on call" to accompany mentally and physically handicapped elementary students of school age on field trips. The staff needed assistance in supervising and keeping track of the children when they left the school building. Central High students not only had an opportunity to learn about the behavior of mentally retarded people in a nonthreatening, unobtrusive way, but they also provided a service and may have helped close the social gap between themselves and the younger, disabled children.

—In a course in "Restaurant Foods," twenty students spent four afternoons visiting and working in a variety of restaurants from fast-food establishments to elegant, gourmet restaurants. They gained an overview of the differences in organization, food preparation, and clientele.

—In an interdisciplinary social studies-science course called the "Web of Life," students spent a full day canoeing down the Mississippi River to gather firsthand data for a study of how the ecological and historical development of the city of Minneapolis was influenced by the river.

—To give one last example, in an advanced German class students prepared and conducted a tour of the Minneapolis Art Institute in German. They gathered information about the history and culture of the German settlements in the region by interviewing residents.

Action-Learning Courses and Programs

The action-learning course or program combines the strongest features of previously examined models into a course that is integral to the school's academic program. The community experience forms the heart and is the central focus of the course, but it is combined with continuing classroom experience with emphasis on providing information, skills, and generalizing principles that directly assist students in interpreting their experiences and help them operate more successfully in their placements. There is a strong assumption in this model: whereas experience *can* be educational, it is neither necessarily nor automatically so. During 1975-76 and 1976-77, approximately 1,700 students participated in action-learning courses. Several descriptions of these courses follow.

At Central High School a course entitled "Student-Community Involvement Project" is offered as a regular social studies option. The class meets for the last two hours of the school day and students receive two academic credits. On three days of the week students report to class and leave immediately for a nearby community center. There they staff a program for senior citizens, providing a variety of services for elderly people in the neighborhood. They perform useful chores (shovel snow, move furniture) for those who still live in their own homes and apartments. This has helped the old and the poor remain in their homes and maintain their independence. Students spend the other two days serving in a nursing residence for the elderly. Once a week the students meet as a class to relate their community service experience to standard subject matter. They may receive information about and discuss senility or other problems often mistaken for senility. They may receive and share specific ideas on things to do when they return to their field placements. They may be given help in improving their observational and data-gathering skills. Time may be spent in writing diaries in which the students reflect on some of the personal implications of their involvement. In short, the classroom experiences may have a variety of formats and focuses, but all relate to, and are integrated with, the community action experiences.

In a course in the home economics department at Southwest Secondary School, students learn about housing, consumerism, and family living through direct experience. The placements for the course include serving internships with real estate companies and interior design studios, helping poor families redecorate and refurbish their homes, or working with a public interest research group investigating unsafe toys. Several students do not leave their home school for their project, but offer cooking and sewing courses to elementary students brought to the school's home economics kitchens by van each day.

In the half-day action-learning alternative program at Bryant Junior High School, community research and service were used to study the overall theme of people, subdivided into three units: the body, the environment, and hunger. To gather original data on the topic of the body, for example, the seventh- and eighth-grade students could choose to teach a Red Cross course on first aid to fourth-graders; interview researchers and specialists on cancer, heart disease, or other diseases; or work in a nursing home. For the unit on environment, one group of students studied whether timber wolves ought to be a "protected" species (first, at the library; then, through interviews; finally, on a trip to northern Minnesota). They then developed a one-hour presentation on wolves, which they gave in elementary schools and high schools around the city. All students in the program learned not only how to use the "city as a classroom," but how to find their way around the city as well. Before venturing out on interviews and field placements, students had to pass a test on the use of Minneapolis city maps and bus schedules.

Two other programs, which deserve much more space than can be given here, utilize two major community facilities, the Minneapolis Institute of RTS and Hennepin County Government Center, as action-learning sites. Both facilities have house programs that provide an integrated learning experience and opportunities for students to interact with community decisionmakers. In the program at the Minneapolis Institute of Arts, students study the future of their city. They meet with the curatorial staff of the museum to examine the artistic and cultural needs of the community. Urban architects help them understand the need for quality design in city planning; governmental officials discuss environmental concerns and energy constraints that will determine the future of urban areas.

The new government center, housing both city and county offices, is the site for a two-hour social studies-English course entitled, "Youth in Pursuit of Justice." The classroom component emphasizes law and American government. Students choose issues of special interest and then investigate them using the human and material resources of the facility. They observe trials in progress, discuss plea bargaining with the city attorney and with judges, attend and participate in public hearings devoted to new city ordinances, see long lines of persons looking for jobs or requesting unemployment compensation. They interview many people. The second phase of this program, which is not yet fully implemented, will involve apprenticeships in governmental offices.

Sequence of Courses and Experiences

We presently have no organized examples of sequenced courses and action-learning experience, but the goal is to develop a rational sequence of courses and community experiences that will help young people gain the skills, motivation, and competencies to make the transition to adulthood effectively. Such a curriculum would extend over a considerable period of time and would provide increasingly challenging experiences through the secondary schools. Programs at both the junior and senior high levels are beginning to develop the sequenced approach. Data are being gathered on the content, duration, and structure of action-learning experiences that seem appropriate to students at various ages and developmental levels.

EVALUATION

Because of the diversity of action-learning experiences offered within the seven schools in Project ACT, it is difficult to provide any comprehensive picture of student and faculty reaction to the project. Some common themes do, however, emerge from student and faculty evaluations of the program.[4]

—To some extent, students developed more positive attitudes toward people different from themselves. The majority of students either held more positive or unchanged attitudes toward classmates of other races, small children, senior citizens, and adults as a result of the action-learning program.[5]

—Students reported that they were most satisfied with the heightened responsibilities that were given them, for example, working in a community placement office without the continuous supervision of a teacher, making appointments with adults for interviews, arranging their own transportation, and so forth.

—Most students reported that they made a significant contribution to the agency or organization in which they volunteered.

—The majority of students and teachers surveyed reported that students gained more knowledge about other groups of people, self-knowledge, ability to get along and work with others, and information about specific careers through action learning than through classroom work alone.

—The majority of students reported an increased ability to learn from their own direct experience, in contrast to learning from books and lectures, a significant finding since the ability to learn from one's own contingent experience is a skill that is critically needed in adult life.

FUTURE PLANS

There is a long-range goal to extend action-learning programs to all secondary schools in Minneapolis, but more immediate objectives are to continue experimenting with a variety of organizational models when adding action learning to the secondary curriculum; to develop a sequence of action-learning experiences that are increasingly challenging from the seventh to the twelfth grade; to refine the means of matching experiences to the student's level of psychological, intellectual, and personal growth. By the end of the project in 1978 there should be a series of program models to guide a variety of students and staffs. Action learning should be neither a reward for excellent students nor a dumping ground for the alienated; it should be integral to the education of all students. In this way it can help fulfill what Herbert Thelen defines as the major function of education: "to induct youth into the community and its way of life."

NOTES

1. Luvern L. Cunningham, "Educational Leadership: The Curious Blend," *Educational Leadership* 33 (February 1976): 323.

2. The six reports are: *American Youth in the Mid-Seventies,* Conference Report of the National Committee on Secondary Education of the National Association of Secondary School Principals, November 30-December 1, 1972 (Reston, Va.: National Association of Secondary School Principals, 1972); *The Greening of the High School,* ed. Ruth Weinstock (New York: Educational Facilities Laboratories, 1973); *Report of the National Panel on High Schools and Adolescent Education* (Washington, D.C.: U.S. Office of Education, 1974); National Commission on the Reform of Secondary Education, *The Reform of Secondary Education: A Report to the Public and the Profession* (New York: McGraw-Hill, 1973); Gisela Konopka, "Requirements for Healthy Development of Adolescent Youth," *Adolescence* 8 (Fall 1973): 291-316; *Youth: Transition to Adulthood,* Report of the Panel on Youth, President's Science Advisory Committee (Chicago: University of Chicago Press, 1974).

3. Arthur Schlesinger, Jr., "What Do We Tell Our Students? Thoughts after Watergate," *School Review* 83 (February 1975): 179.

4. Copies of an external evaluation of the first and second years of the program conducted by the Minnesota Center for Social Research are available from the authors of this chapter.

5. This is a significant result from two perspectives. Since adolescents have a propensity to become more self-protective and more oriented to a narrow peer group or clique for support and acceptance, this change to more open and positive feelings toward those outside their age and social group is important. Second, the experience of school desegregation in the past decade has dramatically illustrated that putting students of different backgrounds in one building does not automatically produce more accepting attitudes toward each other. The program did help students develop more positive feelings toward classmates of different races.

13. Programs for Transition to Adulthood in the Portland Public Schools

Edwin Schneider

The difficulties and problems facing young people as they move from adolescence into adulthood in an increasingly complex and impersonal society become ever more apparent. The work experiences traditionally available to young people in the home, on the farm, or in small communities no longer exist. There is a dissociation of the work place from the home and from smaller communities; there are fewer work opportunities for adolescents; the work available requires more preparation and formal skill development; young people no longer share with their parents the involvement in community activities typical of an earlier time—all raise serious problems for the transition into adulthood.

Portland, Oregon, like most other cities, traditionally isolated students from the community for their formal education, which made transition from high school into the adult world even more difficult. Young people often experience a shock as they move beyond institutional walls to make their way in a world that is quite different from the one described for and perceived by them during adolescence, a shock commonly flavored with disillusionment. Then, by whatever resourcefulness they can muster, adolescents make the transition to the responsibilities, to the decision requirements, to the conflicts, to the hurdles of that world.

It is not difficult to understand why, years ago, the education of students occurred in classrooms. At that time students were faced by so many demands for participation in the adult world that what was most needed was institutional isolation that would allow for academic education. This was a reasonable conclusion in another age and for a quite different society. What is difficult to understand is why the folly of such isolation for a newer age and in a different social milieu was not recognized at least two decades sooner. Even now, probably too few people perceive the need for drastic changes that would allow young people to take on adult roles through the more natural process of interaction with people, with institutions, and with work places already part of the adult world.

In recent years the public has been demanding that education prepare students for careers by the time they graduate from high school. Citizens in Portland have taken seriously the demand that education be oriented toward a career. There is a career awareness program in the early years that encourages young people to explore, in a tentative and preliminary way, some of the characteristics of the world of work. This is largely accomplished through reading and using other materials in the classroom. In the middle grades the design calls for visiting work places as students explore, once again in a tentative and broad fashion, the actual milieu of various careers. Later still, in high school, there is participation through work in career fields. This career orientation is important. It has done much to draw schools out of their parochial views about what constitutes worthy, formal edutional experiences. For the moment, these career programs constitute the major hope for merging the boundaries of the school and the community.

As vital as these experiences may be, they are not broad enough. They do not adequately reflect students' needs to become fully aware of available opportunities, to understand what is involved in each, or to participate in a meaningful way in the diverse institutions, agencies, enterprises, and organizations present in modern society. Too often students become involved only when they will be paid for their work while they are training. This leaves out social and volunteer organizations, offices, commissions, board rooms, hospitals, and literally hundreds of other organizations that together form the fabric and a large part of the essence of social order. These also deserve student awareness and involvement.

In spite of the many Portland students engaged in formal work experience programs, the superintendent of schools and members of the board of education recognized the need to expand the range of the experiences and the number of students involved and to make more flexible the structure in which such experiences could occur. These people recognized that there were rich experiences available outside the walls of school—perhaps, indeed, richer and more valuable than many of the experiences available in school. The board of education moved to grant credit for such experiences, thereby moving from the parochial view that only the school was in a position to conduct programs and provide experiences for which credit toward graduating from high school might be granted.

The board of education further expressed interest and concern by formally adopting a policy directing the administration to develop extensive off-campus learning programs to encourage student participation, to grant credit for such experiences where feasible, and to design mechanisms and procedures to allow for off-campus experiences. This was all to be done, of course, without immense additional cost.

While we had been providing direct staff liaison between the school and work place in the development and supervision of student work experiences, the broad new off-campus thrust was quite beyond the capabilities of that limited staff. This forced a change in the program that may ultimately prove to be one of its strongest features. It became necessary to form an organization of business and other community leaders and educators to develop working relationships designed to increase the involvement of the students in the community and the community in the schools. This organization, called IPAR (Institute for Public Affairs Research), is funded by about $100,000 annually, a sum contributed largely by private businesses.

The organization conducted an inventory of the community-at-large to catalog situations in which students might become significantly involved in a learning process. That inventory was and is still a significant contribution to the program. This effort is further aided by offering university credit and a stipend to teachers who are willing to enroll in a class where the major assignment is to conduct personal interviews with business and organization leaders in an attempt to identify resources available within those groups. This organization and this process will undoubtedly be critical components in any effort to help students find learning situations within the many types of institutions. Several full-time staff members now connect the schools with the community and the community with the schools.

In the early stages of Portland's off-campus programs, it became necessary to design a second significant approach to the problem of involving students in off-campus situations. Without large staffs to go out and do developmental work, to find enough situations, and to provide personal liaison for supervision, students themselves had to identify those institutions and organizations in which they would like to have learning experiences. School departments were asked to designate people on the staff who could best aid the students in exploring their interests and in developing proposals for an off-campus experience. Once the student develops such a proposal, he approaches the institution or organization to determine whether there is a willingness to permit him or her to become involved. If the organization is willing, the student works with that organization to revise the proposal in ways in which that organization might think necessary. After the student goes through the process of negotiating a proposal acceptable to student, parents, organization, and school, the necessary signatures are obtained, and the program becomes operational for that student.

That is still only part of what is required. There must also be a person in the organization who is willing to accept primary responsibility for supervision of the student's work. And, since the school has little direct influence, if any, where the experience occurs, the school must rely upon the negotiated contract, upon occasional conversations with the student, and upon written communications with the supervisor at the place of internship for an evaluation of the student's progress. This requires an abdication of the notion that school personnel are the only ones qualified to make merit judgments on the achievements of students. The internship supervisor is able, on the basis of relatively limited guidelines, to make valid assessments of the degree to which a student has carried out the contract.

Counseling by a member of the staff in the department most closely associated with the area of special interest is useful both to the staff and the student. In time, if enough students are involved in such programs, larger portions of staff time can be diverted to the counseling and liaison relationships. It would be desirable to expand that staff now if funds were adequate, for this would help the program and improve the quality of the experience, apart from the fact that the student and the representative of the organization plan, program, and evaluate the experience and should continue to do so.

Portland students can be found in agencies of the government, in public utilities, in volunteer organizations, in political organizations—the kinds of organizations described earlier as having promise for students. Credit is granted for cultural experiences such as playing in the junior symphony and doing research in the Oregon Museum of Science and Industry. One student who is well along the way toward developing Olympic-level skills in skating is receiving credit for advanced work off campus as a skater since that will undoubtedly be an important part of the student's adult life.

Nor should we overlook the many possibilities that exist within the school itself for students to engage in adult activities. There are many opportunities to participate in the learning process by helping other students or by becoming involved in developing the climate, the organization, and the decisionmaking processes. These are all significant experiences. The capacity to develop in this way has long been present, but many schools are only now beginning to realize that it is possible to do so. The school still lacks the full reality that might be possible as more students become exposed to and involved in diverse organizations in the larger society.

This account of the importance of off-campus programs, some of the experiments, and outcomes that are encouraging is not meant to suggest that the Portland schools have solved the problems of transition from youth to adulthood, that we have found a panacea. Indeed, we are lacking in some major areas of development that are clearly essential. For one thing, better orientation programs are needed for those persons and organizations that participate with the schools and the students in order to provide the kinds of constructive and realistic experiences that the students need. Not only would students benefit more directly from more intensive and more successful orientation, but the relationships between the schools and the organizations, which must be perpetuated over time, could be improved. Then there is the problem of transporting students. In Portland, the board pays the costs on public transit for students who have a financial need. The logistics of transportation can be a significant problem, however, especially for schools in more remote areas.

There are also staffing problems. There must be enough people to provide leadership and guidance in this kind of program, and they must have the kinds of special skills needed to foster the relationship between agencies and students in a highly individualized and considerably different kind of learning structure.

Progress is slow because this is fairly new territory, but progress is being made and there can be no turning back. The goal is to see that all high school students have some prolonged experience, either part of the day over an extended period of time or all day for a shorter period of time, in the world where they are soon to be full-time participants. In this way students can begin to develop insights and perspectives that permit them to move tentatively, gradually, but more certainly toward being able to cope with the complexities of the world in which they find themselves when they leave school.

14. Youth Service Work: An Antidote to Alienation

Mary Conway Kohler and *Bruce Dollar*

Considerable attention has been turned in the recent past to the place of youth in our society and to the process by which they become adults. The advance of technological society has drastically altered the status of young people: where once there were useful outlets for youthful energies in forms that included work on family farms and small businesses and unskilled labor in developing industries, changing economic realities have foreclosed many or most of these outlets. As a result, many young people have been forced to postpone their entry into, or often even their exposure to, adult activities. Today's jobs require greater skills, and the economy and the labor market can now barely support the adult population. The consequent economic marginality of teenage youth (except as consumers) is reflected in an unemployment rate several times higher than that for adults.

To occupy young people during the years before it is able to absorb them as workers, society has expanded the role of the schools. The unfortunate effect has been to isolate adolescents and to delay their learning adult roles, work habits, and skills. Schools traditionally emphasize cognitive development. This is appropriate. Young people do need to know about language, mathematics, history, and science in order to function in the adult world. Yet young people must also learn responsibility, decisionmaking, cooperation with other people, and

Reprinted, with permission, from *The Center Magazine* 9 (May-June 1976): 20-27.

self-management. Such development is usually neglected in schools, even in the nonacademic curricula, perhaps in part because the schools were never intended to perform so broad a function.

Since the schools are limited in the ways they can prepare youth for adulthood, many of the most important needs of adolescents go unsatisfied. For example, young people need to explore adult roles and attitudes in comparatively protected settings where failure can be a source of insight rather than despair. If the transition from child to adult is to occur smoothly, young people must have contact with a variety of adults—not just parents or teachers. And they must have the opportunity for a wide range of experiences in the world of adults. They need to feel the responsibility and satisfaction of being needed by other people. Most of all they need to develop the confidence that comes from achieving self-established goals.

Defining youth as traditional beings who must "wait" until they are "ready" to take on adult responsibilities has come to mean that youth are expected to "do" practically nothing of significance. Not only does this deny the chance to learn by doing—for many the most effective way to learn—but also it frustrates one of youth's most urgent needs, which is to "make a difference" in their environment.

Fortunately, as this situation has grown more acute, responses have formed along several fronts. One approach has been a series of studies of the institutional and societal contexts of the youth that underlie the widely recognized alienation among youth, the needs of young people in contemporary society, and alternative strategies for lessening their alienation and meeting their needs. Virtually all these studies cite the general lack of roles for young people other than the passive, restrictive role of student; the greatly protracted period of "useless" adolescence, by comparison with earlier eras, as young people spend more and more time being schooled in "preparation" for adulthood; and the urgent need of youth for experiences by which to develop social maturity, defining their social values while establishing their own value to society.

A different, more pragmatic kind of response, meanwhile, has been taking place at the grass roots. In many communities and schools across the country, thousands of young people and adults have been devising their own solutions to the predicament of youth. These efforts take a great variety of forms in keeping with their local origins. They are forming the base for a potential movement to afford significant participatory experiences to youth on a large scale. They provide a vital, practical counterpoint to the many more theoretical studies of conditions and needs that have called for just such innovations. The following examples of some of these efforts suggest their range.

Community problem solving. In New York City, young members of the Teenage Tenants Council have learned to spot and report housing violations in their neighborhood. A youth-run ecology organization in San Francisco bought equipment and recycled 2,500 pounds of aluminum in its first year of operation. In Hoffman, Minnesota, students visit regularly the town's nursing home for the aged and an activity center for the mentally retarded; their school compositions reflect their experiences with their institutionalized companions.

Community manpower. In Denver, students at Manual High School build and renovate houses as part of urban redevelopment and inform community residents of redevelopment plans. In Vermont, students in a state-wide program called DUO (Do Unto Others) receive academic credit for work in a wide variety of service and community agencies. Students in Darien, Connecticut, operate an emergency ambulance service. In San Francisco, young people staff the Exploratorium Science Museum.

Entrepreneurship. Teenagers in Cornwall-on-Hudson, New York, created and maintain a natural science museum which provides education and recreation for them, younger children, and the rest of the community. Home economics students in Portland, Oregon, opened a restaurant in their school and prepare daily meals for teachers and students. Fifteen high school students in Fort Knox, Kentucky, serve as elected officers of a student-controlled credit union that has helped students secure loans and save over $41,000 in six years.

Communications. Navajo youth in Utah interview the old people in their tribe and preserve their traditional tales on film and in books. Youth in Washington, D.C., publish their own magazine, *Cityscape,* which explores the history of their urban neighborhood and the lives and occupations of its residents through articles, interviews, and photographs. Junior high school students in Guilford, Connecticut, researched the history of their town and presented it in a booklet entitled "Twelve Spoons and Two English Coats."

Resources for other youth. Students in Hartsdale, New York, run a Rap Room, where young people can drop in for informal counseling by their peers. Youth Advocates, a crisis service in Seattle, Washington, trains teenagers to staff a hot line and rap center for other young people. High school students in Berkeley, California, provide vocational guidance, training in job application skills, and counseling services to their peers.

Curriculum building. A social studies lab cart with multimedia presentations prepared by students was invented and has been operated by students in Enfield, Connecticut, for the past seven years. High school youth in Philadelphia provide a traveling puppet show to educate younger children about the danger of drugs, venereal disease, and alcoholism. Another group of high school students in the same city has developed an environmental curriculum which they use to teach younger children.

The young people in these programs are demonstrating, along with thousands of others, that when given a chance youth can make significant contributions to their communities while meeting their own needs for defining themselves through creative, responsible activities.

Since 1967, the National Commission on Resources for Youth, which was founded expressly to promote opportunities for responsible participation for youth, has sought out these instances of local initiative. Besides acting as a clearinghouse [for] information, the commission has monitored those programs it considered most worthy, helped new programs become established, and operated some demonstration projects of its own. It has adopted the term "youth participation" to apply to those efforts that meet the standards it has set for such programs.

In the course of this work, we of the commission have had our initial belief in the viability of youth participation as a significant remedy for some of youth's severest problems repeatedly confirmed. Youth participation can free young people from the passive, dependent roles enforced on them. When young people are involved in situations where they can make an active contribution to their community, they discover their own strengths and the satisfactions of helping.

Unfortunately, many educators tend to equate work alone with youth participation or action learning. Although work can provide youth with valuable skills and useful insights into the operation of adult society, it can also be as limiting to growth as the worst of traditional school settings. The point of youth participation is not that young people should merely become familiar with the world of work; adulthood involves much more than work. Young people should have access to a range of experiences that helps them to make wise choices about what is best for them and for their community and that permits them to assume a valued role in their community.

Yet if this wide range of potential experiences is to have its full effect in guiding youth toward responsible adulthood, the youth participation programs must be carefully planned and supervised. After observing hundreds of programs, good and bad, the commission has identified several elements that we think are essential for an effective youth participation program. A youth participation program must:

—Maximize decision making by the youth participants. This includes decisions affecting the planning and development of the project itself, as well as decisions affecting the actions of individual youth.

—Address a need that is perceived as real by the young people, . . . not as work invented to keep them occupied. One way to assure this is to have the young people themselves decide upon the need and the activity that will meet it.

—Be respected by the community. Compensation and school credits are examples of concrete evidence that a project activity is taken seriously.

—Include a learning component. . . . Young people receive guidance in interpreting and evaluating their experiences in the participatory setting.

—Offer challenge and accountability. Project activities should not be made simple or "safe" to protect youth from possible failure. In order to cultivate qualities of responsibility and resourcefulness, youth must face authentic and difficult problems and be held accountable for their solutions.

—Promote maturity. Characteristics of maturity that should be exercised include the capacity to make decisions and follow through on their consequences, the capacity to work interdependently with other people, the capacity to convert concern for others into positive action.

—Offer a glimpse of options available to youth in the adult world. Young people experiment with actual adult situations and come to a more precise understanding of their own interests and aptitudes.

—Offer a communal experience of being interdependent with other young people and adults. Working together toward a common goal provides an alternative to the more frequent competitive relationships among peers, or authoritarian relationships with adults; it improves young people's confidence in themselves and their appreciation of other people.

—Provide opportunity for a working partnership between adults and youth. Young people need relationships with adults, other than parents and teachers, who can function as models and informal counselors.

We use these standards at the commission informally to evaluate programs that come to our attention. We also use them as guidelines to assist in the development of new programs. They are not considered to be rigid or exclusionary criteria, however; rather they describe an ideal toward which we encourage programs to strive. Given the diverse and independent quality of these locally originating programs, it would be both unwise and unrealistic to expect many of them to "measure up" to our post hoc standards. Even though the standards are demanding, a surprising number of programs approximate them very well.

The standards also allow for quite a wide variety of program forms, aims, and activities. Programs have been started by teachers or other school personnel, by community youth-serving agencies, by independent or nonaffiliated adults, and by young people themselves, either in their capacity as students or as community youth. They have been based in generalized youth-serving institutions such as schools, colleges, and community youth organizations and in specialized institutions like runaway houses and juvenile detention facilities. Even within these institutions there is room for great diversity. Virtually every school subject, after all, can have a practical participatory component and will be enriched by it. Conversely, any participatory activity can be broadened and deepened in its impact through interpretive reflection. A school-connected youth participation program, for example, may be any one of the following:

—A class in its own right, with credit.
—A unit within an established course (for example, a full-time project of limited duration or one that takes up a portion of weekly class time).
—A free-period or off-hours project, either for credit or not.
—Cooperative arrangement: project run jointly by a person from the school and a person from the community.
—An outside agency operates the program inside a school.
—An outside agency operates the program in the community; students get school credit.
—A semester-off program operated by the school for credit.
—A semester-off program run by an outside agency; students get school credit.
—Other options, not necessarily school related: an outside agency operates the project in the community; youth are paid.

—Same as above; youth are volunteers.
—Youth run their own projects for themselves.

Out of the diversity of possible and actual youth participation programs, four basic approaches appear to be developed most frequently. Classified by type of program activity, these models still allow room for variations in content, institutional setting, and so forth.

Helping service to others. These are projects in which youth meet regularly and face to face with other people in a helping relationship. The "others" may be infants and preschool children, elementary school children, retarded or handicapped children or adults, age peers, hospital patients, or old people. Students typically travel several times a week to the institution (day-care center, elementary school, hospital, nursing home), serving the people to be helped. The activity lends itself to the concurrent experience-based study of the related fields—early childhood, child development, health services, the aged in society, and so forth.

These programs, though they deal in service to others, are noteworthy for their benefits to the youth themselves who often gain dramatically in self-esteem, responsibility, and other dimensions. They also provide what is largely missing in the lives of all too many young people these days: a close relationship with another person. In this way they fill a need we all have in today's impersonal, often depersonalizing, society—the need to be needed and to find expression for one's capacity to be caring for another.

For example, in a program in Hightstown, New Jersey, a small suburban community, twenty-two students at the local high school earn credit for taking part in a youth-tutoring-youth program. They travel four times a week to two elementary schools to tutor children who need extra academic or social attention. Many of the tutors have their own learning problems, so taking responsibility for helping educate a younger child has helped them to improve their own academic skills as well as to develop responsibility and self-confidence. They use materials they themselves have designed to help individual children with reading or math problems. They plan these lessons and also share tutoring techniques and experiences in a weekly seminar at the high school.

One of the high school tutors in their program—a plain, withdrawn girl with problems both at home and at school—spent six months helping a very frightened nine-year-old girl whose family had just moved there from Puerto Rico. Asked what she could say the program had done for her, the tutor replied, "It's helped me open my mind and see the world a little better. I was depressed with everything, failing everything, and all like that. Then I had this girl to help and I said, 'Hey, she needs me'—and I really felt great. If it weren't for Rita, I doubt if I'd still be in school."

Another of the helping service-type programs is the youth helper in [a] day-care program based in [a] Hartford, Connecticut, inner-city high school. Three days a week, fifteen students travel to four different day-care centers where they engage preschool children in learning activities that, again, the students themselves designed. These youth helpers receive credit for combining their fieldwork with a seminar taught twice a week by a high school home economics teacher. In the seminar they learn early childhood development concepts, relating the concepts to their day-care experiences and picking up vital parenting skills in the process.

One of these helpers told what it was like to work at the center by describing the needs of the little ones there: "They need attention that's sincere, mainly someone to talk to, to play with and get along with, who'll be there when they turn around. You know, a friend besides a parent. Also, someone to copy off of, like to say: if he or she does that, I should too. It's like learning without teaching for them. For me, too, come to think about it."

Service to the community. These projects involve a group of young people in an ongoing project activity that has some benefit for the community, in contrast to the helping service-type program, in which the program activity consists of direct contact between youth and the individuals being immediately served.

Public high school students at [the] St. Paul, Minnesota, alternative New City School, for example, are using videotape as an instrument to inform the public and influence decisions on important municipal issues. In one project, representatives from the Minneapolis and St. Paul Tenants' Unions asked students from New City's public service video workshop to help make a tape on renters' rights. The unions supplied the legal information, and the students furnished the technical know-how and the talent. With the direction of two professional video technicians, students have made more than thirty tapes for community agencies. For each tape they do the research, scripting, direction, interviewing, narrating, and editing. Students earn a trimester's social studies credit while learning firsthand about different issues and viewpoints by working with adults in the community.

A different type of community service is provided by *The Fourth Street i,* a community magazine operated entirely by young people on the Lower East Side of New York City. They rely for material on the resources of the neighborhood—an area with a long history as a ghetto for new populations arriving in the United States. The young people have tried to use their magazine as a voice for poor residents of various ethnic groups by interviewing local artists and craftspeople and by printing poetry and artwork by people who live in the community. The young people who publish the magazine interview, edit, translate, take photographs, and do production work. Their magazine has been used as a reading text in elementary and junior and senior high schools.

Social action. Social action projects are defined as those in which the energies of the group are directed toward the achievement of some specific development or change in the community—some observable, tangible result. Some examples are the establishment of a runaway or drug rehabilitation facility, the passage of a consumer protection ordinance, and legal action against industrial polluters.

The West High School Ecology Club in Manchester, New Hampshire—as a specific instance—was formed in 1971 when a group of students began a campaign to clean up the Merrimack River. One student discovered that the discharge for a local meat-packing plant was turning the Merrimack into "Blood River." He and his classmates documented the pollution. Through their investigation, they helped bring legal action against the culprit. West High ecology students also design ecology lessons and teach them to elementary school children, petition for environmental protection legislation, and make environmental testing equipment and show teachers and students from all over New England how to use it.

The Gloucester experiment, another kind of social action youth project, took place when a sculptor residing in a historic Massachusetts town saw in a colonial cemetary—vandalized and overgrown with weeds—an opportunity to use the talent and energy of young people. With his backyard as headquarters, the sculptor recruited a group of local youth along with a few interested carpenters, architects, and teachers, and the restoration began. The young people did everything from manual labor (including landscaping, clearing brush, and straightening headstones) to research and historical documentation.

Eventually the high school in Gloucester agreed to grant students academic credit for their work. Students doing these restorations acquire skills such as surveying and stonecutting while learning history, archaeology, botany, and ecology.

Community internships. In these models, program participants are placed individually with adults at their work place in the community. Each intern is given his or her own responsibility while each also learns about the work of the sponsor or "community teacher." The interns may all meet in a seminar to discuss what they are learning or they may develop individual learning contracts or do their own community projects in conjunction with their placement.

In one such program, junior high and elementary school students at a public-supported alternative school in Evergreen, a mountain town in Colorado, spend at least half a day each week interning with community adults through the school's apprenticeship program. "Apprentices" from the ages of nine to fifteen have carried out responsible duties at an educational television station, at day-care centers, and at a nearby zoo. They have served as "apprentices" to electricians, veterinarians, photographers, store managers, and potters. The purpose of the program is for young people to experience work with adults who are neither teachers nor parents and to learn about the life of their community through firsthand experience.

The Switching Yard, a community-based agency in Marin County, California, provides another example of this kind of program. It is called the Public Affairs Internship Program. Young participants work several days a week alongside decisionmaking people in county agencies dealing with law, prisoner services, child care, public transportation, health, and government. Each young intern learns the workings of his or her placement site, particularly the job of the community teacher at that site. There is also provision for the interns to carry out responsible work of their own at the work site and for a weekly seminar to help them better understand both the work sites and their own roles as interns.

At least one purpose of the program appeared fulfilled when one of the interns, who had chosen to work with a planner for the bus company, reflected, "I guess I got one thing I wanted from this experience, which was to test it out, to see if I could stand working in an office. I found out that I can't, and it's just made me convinced that what I want to do is have a small business—probably a hardware store in northern California—and be my own boss. . . . Volunteering is a little special. You're not being paid, you don't have to be productive, and if you're not interested in the work, you can find out without hurting anyone."

The most extensive of these programs is the national Executive High School Internship Program, now operating in twenty-seven school districts in seventeen states with 2,500 participants annually. More than 7,000 students have gone through the program. These young people have been placed with judges, hospital administrators, lawyers, business executives, government officials, scholars, and other decision-makers. They prepare memos, attend conferences, research special projects—in short, they become immersed in the organizations where they are assigned. "Seven out of eight of today's high school students will be working under executives or adult supervisors in corporations or public agencies," observes the program director. "Therefore it is essential that young people develop some expertise about dealing with organizations while they are still in school."

The above four program "types" are not precise classifications; they are merely convenient devices for putting some order into the wide diversity of programs that may approximate the criteria cited earlier.

Nor by any means do the four types exhaust the possibilities; they are simply the most commonly occurring program forms in the commission's experience. There are many more programs that could not readily be categorized within any of these types. Indeed, it is our belief that meaningful participatory experiences can be integrated into nearly every kind of learning program for youth. There are few subjects in the academic curriculum that do not lend themselves to a practical component that could involve students in responsible activities in their communities. Examples of such application abound, most of them conceived and implemented by the individual teacher or other adult who continues to lead the program.

In addition to these efforts by individuals, a number of agencies have appeared in recent years that serve schools by operating youth participation programs in the community or by helping to place students in participatory roles outside the school. In some cases these agencies supply the learning component, and credit is granted through a contract arrangement with the high school. The [terms] may involve a class period or more every day, or they may involve taking off a full semester to devote full time to the program. In other instances, the outside agency serves a community liaison function, arranging for the placement of young people in community field sites, while perhaps assisting the regular teachers in reorganizing the class format to coordinate with the community experience.

Participatory programs in which youth assume significant responsibility may also, of course, take place within the school. They may provide a helping service, such as peer counseling or job-seeking assistance; or offer a service to the general school community, such as a student-run credit union.

Although progress in extending participatory opportunities to youth has been made in many individual programs, a great deal remains to be done if youth participation is to have an impact on the broad masses of young people. The absence of any coherent national policy concerning youth seems to legitimize a general lack of commitment to positive youth development.

There is cause of hope in the recent, rapidly growing interest in community-based or action learning, but there is also reason for concern. The concept of "experience" as vital to learning appears to be in danger of being embraced willy-nilly, with little consideration for ensuring the quality of that experience. Already youth participation has been characterized by Francis Keppel of the commission's board of directors, as a "runaway horse," a situation which threatens it with a fate similar to previous innovations whose promise was betrayed by being overpopularized, and thus diluted and corrupted. We have seen schools sending large numbers of young people "into the community" with no preparation, no guidance in the selection of their activity, and no opportunity for the guided reflection they need if their community activity is to be a true learning experience. There may be little to do in these programs but menial or trivial work, and little or no support from trained and sympathetic adults. In one program we know of, a single teacher is assigned to place and monitor as many as 850 students at a time. As acceptance of the youth participation idea spreads, efforts aimed at ensuring and maintaining the quality of the allied experience in youth participation programs will need to be pressed with ever-increasing vigor.

Other issues and concerns, meanwhile, will also have to be faced if youth participation is to succeed. It is essential, for example, that it be recognized as a vitally important component in the education of all youth, not just certain segments of them. Youth participation must not become identified either with "problem" students or with achieving students; it must be neither a stigma nor a privilege. Nor must it be a level in any "track." One potential for misuse that must be assiduously avoided is the use of community experience-based programs as a way of throwing troublesome students out of school.

Another problem is that not all adults who deal with youth are capable of allowing them the degree of responsibility they need for the participatory experience to be challenging and growth producing. At the outset, this means careful selection of adult program leaders who do have that capacity, and recognition that any adult involvement must be voluntary. In the longer run, it means training, or retraining—or even detraining—of adults in the skills and attitudes youth participation demands of them.

From work-study and career education to action-learning and experience-based education, many programs have appeared in recent years that try in various ways to put youth in closer touch with the "real world" outside their schools. Youth participation is broad enough and versatile enough to encompass many of the goals and features of these programs. What sets it apart is its insistence on a unique blend of active participation, the exercise of real responsibility with accountability, and provision for guided, critical reflection on experience. In other words, youth participation is based on the assumption that the best way to learn to be a productive adult is to begin practice in adult activity.

As we might expect, the best expressions about what youth participation can offer young people, as well as what young people can accomplish through youth participation, come from the young people themselves. These two statements were made by John, age fourteen, and Emily, age sixteen, but they could have come from any one of the thousands of young people who also have been involved in youth participation programs.

"You see," said John, "part of what we've got to do is help ourselves. Adults have always had the authority, and now kids don't know what to do, even when they have the chance. So, we've got to learn what to do and how to do it. . . . The thing is, now we're getting some say in things, some authority, and we now know what to do with it to bring about constructive change."

"In our town," said Emily, "everything is measured by status symbols: the biggest, the most. There's a lot of fighting and grabbing for the buck. . . . Now, we're getting more people working for something outside themselves, for the betterment of mankind and society. What we're doing is refusing the short-term gains of status and gratification. The gains we're fighting for are long term; they involve living for others, some of whom are not yet born."

15. A Universal Youth Service

Donald J. Eberly

The complementarity of the needs of 3 million unemployed youth age sixteen to twenty-four and society's unmet needs for community and environmental services strongly suggests that a program of universal youth service, in which every youth would be guaranteed the opportunity to serve in a personally meaningful capacity for a specified period of time, for which she or he would receive a stipend, could not only become a cornerstone of national youth policy but could be extremely beneficial to society as a whole. . . . I will examine how such a program worked on the local level when it was tested in Seattle, Washington, beginning in 1973. A description of how it would operate nationally will follow, along with a proposed interim strategy.

A LOCAL YOUTH SERVICE MODEL

The Program for Local Service (PLS), made possible by a million-dollar grant from the federal ACTION agency to the state of Washington, was designed to determine the value of community service performed by young people, the types of youth who would apply and become participants, the efficacy of the self-matching process (to be described later), and the benefits of the experience to the participants. Essentially, the program provided for youth volunteers to serve in ap-

Reprinted, with permission, from *Social Policy* 7 (January-February 1977): 43-46.

proved public or nonprofit organizations (called sponsors), for which they would receive a yearly stipend of $2,970, plus full medical coverage and other benefits. Program regulations further specified that the work performed by PLS participants had to be antipoverty in nature and participants could not replace regular employees.

In early 1973 invitations to apply to PLS were sent to an estimated 80 percent of all eighteen to twenty-five-year-olds (60,000 persons) in the southern portion of Washington's Kings County, including South Seattle and surrounding suburban and rural areas. Special efforts were made to publicize the program in low-income areas. Within two months of the mailing, PLS received 1,694 applications (about 10 percent of those who demonstrated awareness of the program in a survey conducted by telephone four months after the original mailings). The 1,517 applicants deemed eligible on the basis of age, geographic area, and health were invited to join PLS.

With respect to locating community organizations in need of additional service providers, where PLS participants could do meaningful work, approximately 500 potential sponsors were identified in the Seattle area. About half of these applied for PLS volunteers, 34 agencies were found ineligible, and the remaining 221 organizations generated a pool of 1,200 available positions which were listed in a directory compiled by PLS for use in the self-matching procedure. It was agreed that those organizations which became sponsors of PLS volunteers would contribute $150 per person-year to the cost of the program. No potential sponsors dropped out because of this requirement.

The next step was a one-day orientation session attended by 634 applicants at which the program was described, practice was given in interviewing, and applicants completed one-page resumes. By the end of the session, those applicants still interested reviewed the directory of available positions and made appointments for interviews with three potential sponsoring agencies, according to their preference. "Brokers" and "matchmakers" were available to assist in setting up the appointments and to attend the interviews if requested. Finally, applicants received a voucher and memorandum of agreement which were to be taken to the interviews; there agreements could be negotiated on the basis of the sponsor's needs and the applicant's talents and interests. The agreement spelled out the duties of the participant and the supervisory and training responsibilities of the sponsor.

As interviewing proceeded and agreements were reached between applicants and sponsors, they were returned to the PLS office where each agreement was checked by both program manager and legal counsel for compliance with the law and program regulations. Once an applicant's agreement was certified, he or she was invited to a three-day preservice training session, and the year of service began within a few days. Following this selection procedure, 372 persons (or nearly a quarter of the eligible applicants) became PLS volunteers at 137 sponsoring agencies by June 30, 1973—less than five months after the invitations were sent out. Of particular interest is the fact that the socioeconomic profile of the 372 volunteers is virtually identical to that of the 1,517 eligible applicants. When compared with other young people in the Seattle area, PLS participants were more apt to be female, unmarried, low income, minority, better educated, and, most distinctively, unemployed and seeking work.

The outcomes of PLS are significant for a consideration of the universal youth service concept. Nearly two-thirds (62 percent) of the PLS participants completed the full year of service. Of those who left, one-third were "fired" for breaking the agreement with the sponsor; another third left for good reasons, such as getting a better job; and the remaining third left for neutral reasons, such as moving away or having a baby.

In an effort to estimate the economic worth of the services performed by PLS participants, sponsors valued the work done at $2.15 million, more than twice the amount of the ACTION grant that funded the program. Benefits to the participants may be considered in this light: at the time of enrollment in the program, 70 percent of the participants were unemployed and looking for work. Not only did they find work through PLS, [but] two-thirds reported that their PLS experience had influenced their career or educational plans; 63 percent rated PLS experience very valuable for future employment; and 25 percent said they had received or expected to receive academic credit for their work in PLS.*

PLS more than doubled in size the following year with the state paying 40 percent of the budget and the federal government 60 percent. With withdrawal of federal financial support in the third year, PLS

*Evaluation data on the Program for Local Service came from a set of reports prepared by Kappa Systems, Inc., under contract to ACTION. The most comprehensive report by Kappa Systems on PLS is "Applying PLS through CETA: A Summary of Programs and Models."

declined rapidly in size, as the state was unable to assume the full financial burden.

As an observer of the PLS experience, I found the major lessons for an expanded nation-wide program to be:

—Universal youth service can be justified economically on the basis of the value of service rendered.

—The benefits to the participant would probably be even greater than the average value of services rendered. These benefits include the greatly increased chance of getting a job and the sense of direction acquired for one's life, as demonstrated by the personal testimonies telling of the richness of the experience.

—A program in which opportunities for service were universally guaranteed would attract young people from all walks of life, with a somewhat higher proportion of persons who were low-income and unemployed.

—Universal youth service would become a much-needed rite of passage for many young Americans. It would be a time of testing and assuming adult responsibilities.

How do we move from a local program with a few hundred participants to one at the national level with several hundred thousand, possibly as many as a million or more? The next section outlines the governing principles and a model for such a program, and the final section describes immediate steps that can be taken to maximize youth service opportunities.

A NATIONAL MODEL

Following the local demonstration [program] described above, a nation-wide universal youth service (UYS) model can be proposed which would foster the provision of needed human, social, and environmental services and at the same time benefit greatly the development of youth. It would enable them to gain experience in careers of interest to them, offer cross-cultural and out-of-classroom learning experiences, including practical problem solving, working with people, and the acquisition of specific skills, and, not least, imbue youth with a sense of self-worth and community pride. To accomplish these aims requires attention to certain important features of the program.

UYS must truly be open to all young people in the suggested eighteen to twenty-four age group, with a summer service program for fif-

teen- to seventeen-year-olds. This age range was not selected according to a particular theory as to when youth begins and ends, but to ensure that anyone reaching adulthood has had suitable opportunities to participate in a youth service program. Being truly open also means paying special attention to people who have few skills, are poorly or inadequately educated, are bashful, or do not get along easily with others. Any special services provided should not have the effect of separating these people from others who have the desired skills. For example, persons with few skills may do well at environmental conservation camps where they will serve with college-educated environmentalists and receive necessary training. Persons insufficiently educated with regard to health services may work on health or rescue teams along with persons with more education and experience. Those who are shy may need only the services of a friendly facilitator to assist in the first few interviews en route to finding the right position.

In addition, because seemingly neutral procedures of recruitment and application can develop into overtly or covertly discriminatory practices, the federal government must retain the right of review and have the authority to order rectification.

Successful development of UYS requires a transition period of about three years. The transition period serves two vital functions. First, it allows time for UYS to grow from an idea to a program involving a million or more persons. Various studies suggest that while the need for youth service workers is on the order of 4 to 5 million, the number of openings that could be filled in the next three months is not more than 250,000. It will take some time to translate national or local needs into actual positions with organizations. Another constraint on rapid growth is the size of the supervisory staff. While time demands vary greatly, the typical supervisor may expect to spend two hours per week with the UYS participant, perhaps several hours during the first week or two. Few supervisors can handle more than two or three UYS participants in addition to their regular jobs. This ratio is a limiting factor to agencies' acceptance of UYS participants until the next budget cycle permits the hiring of additional supervisory staff.

Second, the build-up period provides for experimentation within the overall program guidelines. The decentralized administration will permit, even encourage, the states and cities to test a variety of approaches for implementing the goals of UYS. There are many ways, for example, in which UYS participants can derive educational benefits from the UYS experience. These need to be closely watched during the early years of the program to determine which should be incorporated into UYS and to determine the extent to which educational arrangements should remain flexible.

Participation should be arranged by a contract voluntarily entered into by all parties. The contract would describe the responsibilities of the UYS participant, the supervisor, the sponsoring agency, and the funding agency. This approach would extend the choices open to applicants as well as to sponsors, minimize the possibility of misunderstanding among the parties, and establish a reference point for evaluation of the program.

UYS must be based soundly on the need for having services performed. Most of its potential for youth development would vanish if the work were not needed or if the UYS participants perceived the work to be of no consequence. A mandatory financial contribution by the sponsor, as was done in the PLS, would help to emphasize the worth of their service.

Maximum local support of UYS should be encouraged, with underwriting guaranteed by the federal government. Past experience suggests that most cities and states would opt for maximum federal funding. Still, there is much evidence in recent legislation showing that lower levels of government will have discretionary authority over substantial amounts of money for the purpose of meeting social needs. Following the underwriting approach, federal funds would not replace other funds already available, but would be adequate to guarantee service positions to all young people who wanted them. Funds would be administered by state and local governments after being obtained from the federal government through grants. This method has the advantage of fostering local initiative while retaining basic program design.

Persons should be allowed to serve in UYS for no more than four years. A part of the UYS mission is to provide a transition into the world of work, not a lifetime job. However, it would incorporate certain features to facilitate the postservice employment and continuing education of its participants. First, UYS should be a source of information about jobs and education. This information could take the form of newsletters, job information sheets, opportunities for counseling, and referrals to such other agencies and institutions as the employment service and the community education work councils proposed by Willard Wirtz. Second, UYS should certify the work performed by its participant. The certification should be of a descriptive nature, not a judgmental one. Such a certificate should enable the outgoing participants to get beyond the initial hurdle to jobs for which they are qualified. Third, consideration should be given to offering UYS participants an educational entitlement, a "GI Bill for community service," along the lines proposed by Elliot Richardson and Frank Newman in 1972. This could prove a valuable incentive for participation in UYS. Fourth, the Women in Community Service and Joint Action for Community Service programs of the Job Corps should be adapted for utilization by UYS. These programs utilize low-income volunteers to recruit, counsel, and place Job Corps enrollees.

PROGRAM COSTS

Payments of participants would consume most of the money spent on UYS. How should the level of payments be determined? If all young people are entitled to serve, the stipends must be sufficient so that nobody is kept out of UYS because of payments below the subsistence level. On the other hand, payments should not be so high as to be competitive with salaries for comparable jobs in the open market, whether in the public or private sector. A third criterion that would be consistent with the service ethic would be to have no payment differentials based on the jobs done, nor on the qualifications of the participants. Variations in stipends would be dictated by the local cost of living and by the provision of such essentials as food and lodging.

Experience with PLS suggests that a benefit package equivalent to the minimum wage (now $4,784 per year for work weeks of forty hours) is required. When total payments fall below the minimum wage by several hundred dollars, some participants can be expected to dip into their savings, moonlight, borrow money, or resign.

Administrative costs can be held to 15 percent of participant stipends at the beginning of the program and should fall to 10 percent within three years. Several features of UYS lead to this low level of administrative costs: basic supervision and in-service training and transportation costs would be the financial responsibility of the sponsor; preservice orientation and training conducted by the UYS grantee would take only two days at a cost of $100 per trainee; and sponsors would contribute $200 per person-year of service.

Finally, the unforeseeable demands of five or ten years in the future might be better anticipated if sufficient experimental funds—say, 5 percent of the total UYS budget—were devoted to testing new forms of youth service programs. These could range from Canada's Opportunities for Youth to Israel's several models of youth involvement. The Student Originated Studies program sponsored by the National Science Foundation might serve as a model for youth-initiated projects. Also certain cultural and public works projects falling outside the standard UYS criteria could be tested under the experimental program.

AN INTERIM STRATEGY

Because implementation of a national youth service could be delayed by the two to three years required to create a new agency to administer it, a more immediate strategy would be to use those programs already existing or legislated to serve the youth service functions outlined above. The programs that could be adapted for this purpose are the Youth Conservation Corps (YCC), the Young Adult Conservation Corps (YACC), and the Program for Local Service, described above.*

YCC is already a cooperative program with responsibility and funding shared equally between the Departments of Agriculture and Interior. It is also a two-tiered program, with YCC participants engaged in conservation projects both on federal and state lands. YCC would offer the summer service experience for fifteen- to seventeen-year-olds noted earlier, and also provide information on service opportunities once they reach eighteen.

YACC** would offer full-year service opportunities to eighteeen- to twenty-three-year-olds as well as to those sixteen- to seventeen-year-olds who have completed high school or who have dropped out for reasons unrelated to entering YACC. Like the YCC, it is to be administered by the Departments of Agriculture and Interior and is to undertake conservation projects on both federal and state lands.

An expanded PLS would be the vehicle for two essential functions: (*a*) to provide community service opportunities locally, and (*b*) to serve as a recruitment and placement entity for young people wishing to enter the environmental or community service program. With suffi-

---

*Even after the inception of the UYS program, the Peace Corps, VISTA, Teacher Corps, College Work-Study Program, Job Corps, and youth corps programs funded by the Comprehensive Employment and Training Act would remain in effect. After three years of UYS operation, all these programs should be examined to determine the extent to which their functions can be consolidated.

**The YACC passed the House on May 25, 1976, by a vote of 291-70. The Senate tabled the bill on September 15, 1976.

cient funding, and the necessary integration among ACTION and the Departments of Interior and Agriculture accomplished by executive order, it would be possible, through these programs, to guarantee service positions to all interested young people.

A second tier of federal programs can also assist in the development of UYS. The humanpower programs of the Department of Labor, funded under the Comprehensive Employment and Training Act, can provide supervisors and trainers for persons in PLS, YACC, and YCC. The juvenile justice and law enforcement programs of the Department of Justice can be tapped by PLS sponsors to provide supervisors as well as the sponsor's $200 contribution. The same is true of various programs in the Departments of Commerce, Housing and Urban Development, and Health, Education, and Welfare. This dynamic tension among federal funding sources will help to preserve accountability, for each of the funding sources will want to see its purposes accomplished.

In conclusion, it must be remembered that if we continue to procrastinate in dealing with the problem of youth unemployment, there is a good chance that a crash program which is hurriedly assembled and inefficiently managed will be imposed out of necessity. The interim model for a universal youth service proposed here can serve as a test of the UYS concept in beginning to address the problem of youth unemployment, among others. The assessment and refinement of the model over a three-year period can be used to frame full legislative authority for the successful implementation of a universal youth service in this country.